PRAISE FOR NOT ALONE

Living in a spiritually mismatched marriage represents one of the greatest challenges a couple can face. Lynn Donovan and Dineen Miller tackle the issue head-on with grace, honesty and a wealth of practical advice. I'm encouraged by their willingness to reach out to this often-overlooked segment of the Church.

Jim Daly
President, Focus on the Family

I was raised in a spiritually mismatched home and my own mother would have LOVED the wisdom, encouragement and practical help Lynn and Dineen offer in *Not Alone*. Raising children and tackling teens is hard enough in any environment but Lynn and Dineen offer help and hope so you always feel you are NOT ALONE!

Pam Farrel
Author of *Becoming a Brave New Woman, Men Are Like Waffles, Women Are Like Spaghetti* and *10 Best Decisions a Woman Can Make*

Pick up your favorite highlighter because *Not Alone* is one of those rare books full of practical wisdom that you will want to read, reread, bookmark and highlight. While this book is aimed at parents in spiritually unequal marriages, Lynn and Dineen offer godly insight and encouragement for *all* parents. I finished this book feeling, as a sometimes worried mom, that I'm not alone, that my earnest prayers can move God to act, and that He always has my back.

Susy Flory
New York Times bestselling author and a mom of two

This dynamic duo's use of Scripture, prayers, transparent real-life stories and personal study questions is powerful. They have truly walked through the valley that women in spiritually mismatched marriages are in and they offer a firm hope. This is a must-read for women who are seeking wisdom and guidance as they raise their children in the midst of marital challenges.

Courtney Joseph
Author of *Women Living Well* and WomenLivingWell.org

For every mother who has silently wondered, *Am I enough?* authors Lynn Donovan and Dineen Miller point you to the very One who is. You don't have to be in a spiritually mismatched home to appreciate their wisdom and tender companionship on this holy ground called "motherhood." If I could place this book in the hands of mothers everywhere, I would.

Joanne Kraft
Author of *Just too Busy—Taking Your Family on a Radical Sabbatical*

When I think of Lynn Donovan and Dineen Miller, these are the words that come to mind: *sincere, passionate, godly, humble and accessible.* If you're in a spiritually mismatched marriage and you worry about your kids, you've come to the right place. These girlfriends will wrap you up in a hug, they'll tell you the truth and they'll point you to Jesus. They were so right to title this book *Not Alone* because when you're done reading, you'll know and believe that you're not alone on this journey; God is with you and He's got you.

Susie Larson
Radio Host, Speaker, and Author of *Your Beautiful Purpose*

I've walked the road of being in a spiritually mismatched marriage. When I was in my most desperate time of clinging to God, my kids' father was running away. Oh how I wish I would've had *Not Alone* to hold in my hands to combat that feeling of desperation and isolation. With comfort, grace and been-there wisdom, Lynn and Dineen will walk you through with hope—not only for you, but for your kids as well.

Kathi Lipp
Author of *21 Ways to Connect with Your Kids* and *Can I Get Some Help Here—Prayers and Practical Steps When Your Kids Don't Go According to Plan*

I have high hopes for my kids—but perhaps the greatest hope of all is that I want them to know and love Jesus in a way that's authentic and real. Dineen Miller and Lynn Donovan clearly understand the heart's desires of moms like me. *Not Alone* gives moms a resource of practical help and warm encouragement so that they can prayerfully and practically raise kids who not only know Jesus, but also love Jesus wholeheartedly.

Erin MacPherson
Author of *The Christian Mama's Guide* series

Having spent a lot of time as the spiritual leader in my own home, I know how lonely it can feel. *Not Alone* is an invigorating source of hope and grace that calls women to godly parenting and guides them as they entrust their children's spiritual well-being to the Father, the ultimate parenting partner.

Nicole O'Dell
Founder of Choose NOW Ministries and host of Choose NOW Radio

Passing down faith to your children is especially challenging when only one parent believes. Yet, as the title says, you are not alone! These authors and mothers know exactly what you're going through. They can help you navigate the years ahead with hope, grace and clarity.

Arlene Pellicane
Author of *31 Days to a Happy Husband*

I love this book! Lynn and Dineen don't just encourage women—they *empower* them to raise faith-focused children in a secular world. Their excitement is contagious—their wisdom runs deep. Whether you're a single mom or in a mismatched relationship, *Not Alone* is chock-full of practical insight for passionate parenting.

Darlene Schacht
Author of *The Good Wife's Guide* and coauthor of the *New York Times* bestseller *Reshaping It All*

In *Not Alone*, Dineen Miller and Lynn Donovan weave biblical insight together with their own stories as they help mothers discover hope, faith and courage to not only leave a legacy of faith as they passionately parent their children, but also to understand they are not alone in their journey. Although written for women who are in spiritually unequal marriages, are single moms or widowed moms, *Not Alone* will benefit all moms who read it. This is a great resource for small groups and I'm honored to recommend it.

Stephanie Shott
Author, speaker and founder of The M.O.M. Initiative

LYNN DONOVAN
& DINEEN MILLER

Permit the children to come to Me; do not hinder them; °for the kingdom of God belongs to such as these.

—JESUS CHRIST (MARK 10:14, NASB)

Not Alone

Trusting God to Help You Raise **Godly Kids** In a Spiritually Mismatched Home

Regal

For more information and special offers from Regal Books, email us at subscribe@regalbooks.com

Published by Regal
From Gospel Light
Ventura, California, U.S.A.
www.regalbooks.com
Printed in the U.S.A.

Library of Congress Cataloging-in-Publication Data

Donovan, Lynn.
Not alone : trusting God to help you raise Godly kids in a spiritually mismatch home /
Lynn Donovan and Dineen Miller.
pages cm
Includes bibliographical references and index.
ISBN 978-0-8307-6713-7 (trade paper : alk. paper) 1. Parenting—Religious aspects—Christianity.
2. Child rearing—Religious aspects—Christianity. 3. Mothers—Religious life.
4. Non-church-affiliated people—Family relationships. I. Miller, Dineen. II. Title.
BV4529.18.D66 2013
248.8'45—dc23
2013021286

Rights for publishing this book outside the U.S.A. or in non-English languages are administered
by Gospel Light Worldwide, an international not-for-profit ministry. For additional information,
please visit www.glww.org, email info@glww.org, or write to
Gospel Light Worldwide, 1957 Eastman Avenue, Ventura, CA 93003, U.S.A.

To order copies of this book and other Regal products in bulk quantities,
please contact us at 1-800-446-7735.

To Brad and Caitie, Rachel and Leslie,
and to our Abba Father,
who holds all of us in the palm of His hand.

Contents

Acknowledgments

Dear Reader, we want to thank you. So many of you have walked this spiritually mismatched journey with us from our first book, *Winning Him Without Words*, and from our ministry site, www.SpirituallyUnequalMarriage.com. We have watched God turn our online presence into a beautiful community that was birthed out of common trials and challenges and is now moving forward into victories, stronger faith and deeper relationship with our amazing Savior Jesus.

In that beautiful growth God brought us together with our multi-talented editor Kim Bangs, an amazing woman who is a font of inspiration and a blessing to all she meets. We are privileged to call her a dear friend too. And from this friendship has come a stunning relationship with our publisher, Regal Books/Gospel Light. Their staff is a sensational group of people—Bill Grieg, Stan Jantz, Tasha Ruffing, Jackie Medina, Mark Weising, Rob Williams, Carol Eide and the entire sales staff, just to name a few. This amazing team has prayed over us and committed its time and energies to support us and our ministry. Each of these people walks with heartfelt conviction and true callings to serve God in their unique talents. We are so incredibly blessed by them.

And as in our first book, we could not move forward without the approval of our family, out of respect and love for them. Our children—Rachel, Leslie, Brad and Caitie—have eagerly shared stories and reminders with us, their sometimes forgetful moms, about how God has shown up in the funniest of places—in the car ride home, in a home full of love and tacos, in a sock fight, and in so many tears and hugs. God has been so incredibly faithful to us.

As we've walked the path of motherhood, our appreciation for our own mothers has increased tenfold. These two precious women have spoken words of love, have shed tears of joy and pain, and have prayed over us through the years. Both of us are so grateful to our mothers, each of whom took the negatives of her past and determined to make them positives in her daughter's future. To our moms, you are such an inspiration to us.

And finally, we save the best for last, because who knows better how to finish things than our precious Lord and Savior Jesus? Lord, thank You for this amazing journey that continues to astonish and astound us. You are truly the beginning and the end. Thank You for allowing us to be an integral part of the middle. We adore You.

Foreword

How ever you got here, here you are. I know this sounds a bit like a Suessism but it is simply truth. At times we all find ourselves wondering, *How did I ever get here?* But the how isn't the question. The question we should ask ourselves is, *What will I do now that I am here?*

How you came to be raising your amazing children in a spiritually mismatched relationship isn't the issue you need to be most concerned about. Dear friend, simply ask yourself, *Now what will I do?* Or even better, *How now shall I live?*

Parents come in all varieties: single, married, blended, adoptive, foster . . .but all are still parents. And all face the same truth—parenting is hard work! For those who are parenting and missing a spiritual connection with the other parent, the challenge is even greater.

If you are holding this book, I know two things about you already: (1) You are committed to honoring Christ in the way in which you raise your children, and (2) You are much tougher and much more able than you think.

You, friend, are a lot like the two authors of this book.

A few years ago at a writer's conference I led a workshop on developing great proposals that would cause publishers to sit up and take notice. Later that afternoon I had a fifteen-minute appointment with one of the attendees—one that would change my life forever.

When Lynn Donovan sat down to talk to me about the book she and her coauthor, Dineen Miller, were proposing, I was immediately impressed by their passion for the audience of the book—women just like them who find themselves (for whatever reason) in spiritually mismatched relationships. Long before either of them had thought of or dreamed of writing a book, they had developed a web-based ministry for these women—an already well-established ministry that has continued to flourish over the years since Lynn and I met.

I received the proposal, did my prep work, prayed up a
storm and walked into Regal's publishing board meeting ready
to present it. I believe I uttered two sentences from my well-
prepared presentation before two of our sales associates—both
women, on the phone from other parts of the country—offered
their thoughts on what a great need there is in the church to
minister to these women, and how many women are in this
situation . . . and on and on they went. Gratefully, our team
agreed to offer a contract to Lynn and Dineen for their first
Regal book, *Winning Him Without Words*.

In the process of working on the first book, I learned that
Lynn and Dineen had never actually met in person! So I
arranged for them to come to my hometown, meet me, some
of our team, some of my friends and each other!

After meeting Dineen I saw the same passion in her for
ministry that I had seen in Lynn. These two are "cut from the same
cloth," as it were. They don't write from a place of observation,
they write from a place of life experience. Both are married to
amazing men who have yet to take up their spiritual journey.
However, their marriages, not without challenges, are thriving.

Not only have Lynn and Dineen both journeyed down
the path of a spiritually mismatched relationship, they have
each raised two children while doing it—children who have
encountered life along the way, have had struggles and yet are
thriving. You'll read much more about their children in the
pages of this book.

Again, this is not a book written by two field experts or
those who have observed women in spiritually mismatched
relationships. These two women live life (very well) in the
trenches alongside you each and every day.

You will find rich food from the Word of God in these
pages and prayers to help your heart as you call out to God for
wisdom, but you'll also find transparency, vulnerability and
such practical wisdom that you will close the book knowing
you can thrive too!

It is an honor to partner with Lynn and Dineen in their
mission to develop a community of support and prayer for
women in spiritually mismatched marriages. Since the time we

reviewed their first proposal, we have been astounded by the ways God has used them to bless others. Doors have opened before them to reach more and more and God has given them incredible opportunities to share the truth. I feel like we've only begun to see what God will do.

Has this all happened because Lynn and Dineen are so special? (And they are.) No, it is because they realized, as you will too, that . . .

- The first order of life is to be committed to honoring the Lord.
- The second is to see that God has equipped you with what you need to do the task at hand.
- And, of course, the third is to step out in faith and do it!

As close to seven billion of us now journey through life on this tiny planet, I am grateful every day that by God's grace and plan our three lives intersected. As I mentioned, my first meeting with Lynn changed my life forever. I didn't know it at the time but I do now. As honored as I am to partner with them to get their messages out in book form, I am much more honored and humbled to call these two amazing legend women of God my friends and fellow prayer warriors.

You dear sister are not alone—never, ever, ever alone. The God who created the universe walks with you each and every day. He will give you what you need to thrive. Wisdom, miracles, friends—all you need He will amply provide.

On this journey, no matter our circumstances, we are truly NOT ALONE!

From one of the seven billion on the journey,

Kim Bangs
Senior Manager, Regal Books

Introduction

Her children arise and call her blessed; her husband also, and he praises her: "Many women do noble things, but you surpass them all."
PROVERBS 31:28-29

You are joining us for an incomparable journey. We, the authors, are linking arms with you as we walk with our Savior and our children into the Promised Land. We are ordinary women, who love our kids, our unbelieving husbands, and we love Jesus. We are just like you. We are living out our faith in front of the eyes of our family. We are trusting our Lord to bring our spouse and our children home to a vibrant and personal relationship with Jesus.

If you've picked up this book, you are likely living in a spiritually mismatched relationship to some degree. Spiritual discord exists between you and your husband or, perhaps for some, an ex-husband; or perhaps you are standing alone in faith as a single mother. We welcome you into an amazing and unique family of God: the spiritually mismatched. There are actually many of us traveling this path. We support each other, pray for one another and love each other. We love one another through the transforming power of Jesus in our lives. We are thrilled you have found us, and we hope you will join this amazing community through our online ministry, www.MismatchedandThriving.com.

This ministry was set in motion in 2006, when Lynn followed God's leading to start the blog *Spiritually Unequal Marriage*. Around this time God brought the same calling to Dineen's heart and led her to Lynn. God knew what He was doing, as the two of us have become best friends, prayer warriors for one another and ministry partners. We share this ministry with all of you, bringing practical wisdom, hope and God's truth to wives and mothers. Ultimately, our purpose is to bring honor and glory to the Lord and to His Son, Jesus.

Starting today, find rest in the fact that you no longer have to walk this crazy path of being spiritually mismatched alone. Many have gone before you, and there are more of us a few steps behind. But we all need each other, and through our love and faith in God, we can thrive in our mismatched-dom.

And so can our children.

We have walked where you have walked. With Jesus at our side, we've experienced victories in our marriages, and we are witnesses to the triumphs within our children even as we wait for our husbands to come to faith in Christ. In our first book, *Winning Him Without Words: 10 Keys to Thriving in Your Spiritually Mismatched Marriage*, we share our hope for our marriages. If you are struggling in your mismatched marriage, we pray that you will find healing and hope in its pages.

As for the book you now hold, *Not Alone*, it was born out of our great passion for mothers and children.

As women who are married to unbelieving spouses and who are alone in faith in our marriages, it is very much part of our journey to pray and to stress over our spouses' salvation. But right behind that "Goliath," we worry a great deal about our children's faith walk. We ask ourselves, "Will my husband's lack of faith impact my child's decision to follow Christ?" Or, "Am I enough to raise my kids to faith all by myself?" We camp on these questions.

A lot.

But, my friends, this journey will prove that a mere woman can be a giant killer. Goliath has nothing on us. We will discover together that ordinary mothers are God's chosen vessels to bring faith to the generations. In this book we will walk through God's Word, uncovering His promises to us as mothers as well as His promises for our children. We will view our parenting in a new light and witness God's faithfulness to us, to our kids and to a world in desperate need of hope.

On this crossing toward the land of promise, we will offer you some practical tips on how to capture teachable moments for eternity. We will share with you some stories of how we taught our kids the value of prayer, and we will give you ideas about how to share God's Word with your kids. We will talk about some of the pitfalls of parenting—those snakes of doubt or fear that sneak around our houses—and we will cross into the land of milk and honey as we recognize the triumphs that come through the faithfulness of a mother's love.

Each chapter provides a key principal that will help you pass your faith on to your children. And, at the end of each chapter, we have included a "Discovery" section with questions designed to help you grow closer to Christ and to grow as a parent, a "Prayer" segment to help empower you through the love of Christ in your parenting efforts and, finally, a "Respecting Dad" paragraph.

At the back of the book are additional resources for you to use on this journey: some thoughts on "Rebellion and the Prodigal Adult," a Scripture index of verses about our identity in Christ, a compilation of prayers that you can pray for your kids, a collection of fun family-faith projects for your family to enjoy, and a leader's guide for using this book in small-group settings.

At the time of the writing of this book, our children are entering into young adulthood. We have parented our kids in the trenches of mismatched parenting throughout their lives. And we two moms are God's proof that ordinary women can thrive in a spiritual mismatch as we raise our children to know God in a home in which faith in Jesus is not embraced by two parents.

We greatly desire to come alongside you and share what God has graciously given to us: healing for our marriages and hope for our children. And we pray with fervor that you will discover the power and authority we as believers have through Christ to live a life of purpose, significance and joy. And most of all, we pray that you are the greatest influence upon your children, growing them in faith, hope and love and ultimately into a lifelong relationship with Jesus.

This journey we are taking together is all about raising our children to faith. In this book you will face some of your deepest fears, but you will read much more about the power of a mother's love. This is a parenting book, but it's much more.

Lynn Donovan and Dineen Miller

It's a love letter to all mothers—a message of love that changes our homes, our kids and our lives. It's about the Father's love, which impacts those around us and changes ordinary moms into women of extraordinary grace, beauty and wisdom.

Travel with us, because when you reach the end of this book, you will parent with a new confidence and boldness through the love of our Father. You will be mothers who change your world, impact your children for all eternity, and reveal Jesus to those around you. You are the ordinary moms who will bring faith to the generations.

We have prayed for you with an earnest heart. We have asked the Lord to move in your life and in the lives of your children. We have asked for the salvation of everyone in your home. We bring this book to you with the sincere hope that you see Jesus on every page.

With hearts filled with eternal love for you,

Lynn Donovan and Dineen Miller

Lynn's Story

I'm an ordinary mom and an ordinary wife just like you. I have been a mom for more than 30 years. In fact, I've been parenting longer than I have done anything else. I've raised kids for more years than I worked in corporate America. I've been mothering for more years than I was a child growing up in my parents' home and even longer than I've been married. Yep, I have a crazy and mixed-up story. And I'm finding that I'm not alone. Many of you, like me, have raised or are raising children in a not-so-traditional home. And if you've picked up this book, you are likely one of those women. My friend, I know how you feel. I know your doubts, and I've felt the pressure and fear that we mothers struggle through when it comes to raising our children.

So sit with me for a while. I am a mom who understands your struggles. I have walked in the parenting trenches for a long time, and I have experienced firsthand the powerful love and faithfulness of our God. My parenting journey has meandered through divorce, single parenting, remarriage, a blended family and several more obstacles, which I will share with you later in this book. God has allowed me the experience of being a single mother who, after paying the bills and having only 25 dollars remaining to my name, was able to stretch it for two weeks until the next paycheck. I've experienced the difficulty of grappling with a shared-custody arrangement. But as I look back on all these experiences, I see how the Lord has used them all to shape me and my children for my good and His glory. We serve a God of great redemption and my story is filled with this truth. My past challenges and circumstances of raising a child in today's culture created in me a heart full of empathy for mothers.

I think my mismatched chronicle began in earnest a few years after I married my husband, Mike, at the end of a long tour in the badlands of the prodigal nation. The story of the prodigal son in Luke 15:11-32 remains one of my most beloved stories from God's Word and one to which I easily relate.

I was raised in a Christian home. Thinking back to my growing-up years, though, I believe that my childhood faith was more a relationship with church than with Jesus. In my early 20s and lacking a firm faith foundation, I ran far away from my Sunday School background. I abandoned my faith, choosing to live a life in which the only god that existed was me. I made many wrong turns during my prodigal wanderings. I divorced, thus becoming a single mom raising my then-eight-year-old son alone. Not long after my divorce, I met my second husband at a bar in Las Vegas. Yep, what a great way to start a relationship. So if you've made a few mistakes—ahem, I mean blunders—in your life, I "get" you. And if you haven't, please be patient with me, because God likes to work with all of us—short, blonde, prodigal girls like me as well as those kids who never wander from the farm.

Three years into my second marriage, the Jesus of my youth began to woo me back to Himself. I heard His call. My heart soared, and I went running home to the outstretched arms of Christ. I share a lot more about my early years of marriage in our book *Winning Him Without Words*. But suffice it to say, when I first came back to Christ, my husband was not very happy about the new Man in my life.

To be fair to him, my husband had also become an instant father to my son when we married. And the year that I stepped into this journey of living unequally yoked, I also became pregnant with our daughter. Whew! Talk about a lot for both of us to navigate. And, my friends, it's a good thing that Jesus showed up, because I needed to lean on Him. And lean on Him I did.

I have parented a child through divorce and through shared custody. I've faced terrifying times in which my son was outside my influence, protection and control. I have parented my daughter with a daddy who was a proclaimed atheist. I have fixed boo-boos, wiped snotty noses, prayed with fervor for my children's faith, cried heavy tears, giggled with glee, and kicked a soccer ball and played Barbies more times than I can remember. I have caught my breath as each of my children have walked out the door with car keys in hand to drive to school for the first time, they not knowing that they took every piece of my heart with them as they drove away. Mostly I have loved two little people more than I thought was humanly possible.

The privilege of becoming a mother is absolutely the best gift God has ever given me. I've gained understanding of what God desires for all of us: a childlike faith. Through mothering I experienced the joys of discovery as my children grew, as they forged their own stubborn or carefree personalities. My heart soared when each of them were baptized. And I turned red faced and hid under the pew at church when my son, age five, blurted out in front of the entire church after the Christmas pageant, "There's fire on my butt."

Ahem.

The church exploded in uncontained hysterics. And to this day I still don't know why he said what he said.

Ah . . . the mysteries and hilarity of raising children.

It's always exciting. Your heart is always engaged. You will never stop caring, loving and praying. These special and purposeful relationships with our children are God's intentional design. And it is good.

The joy of mothering fills my heart every day. I'm humbled that God found me worthy to parent two children into adulthood. And yet I have agonized over my own confidence and asked myself, "Am I doing this parenting thing right?" And now, as the youngest of my children finishes her senior year in high school, I ponder the scariest question of all: Will she choose Jesus? Has my husband's unbelief influenced her to abandon her faith as an adult? Will she walk the prodigal path? Or will she embrace her childhood faith and make it her own?

Those questions are yet to be answered, but one thing I know for certain: God loves my two kids with a passion and a purpose that I can't begin to fathom. He has a plan to prosper them and not to harm them, plans to give them hope and a future. And He has the same plans for us as mothers.

God has always been a faithful parent to my children. He protected them when I couldn't. He loved them when they needed it most. He laughed with them in the sun and kissed the tears from their cheeks when they were sad. He was an ever-present help, comfort and advisor. He was and always has been Abba Father to my children. And with God leading our home through an imperfect mother and in spite of an unbelieving dad, my kids are going to be just fine. How do I know? Because they rest in the powerful hands of an all-loving God. I will do my part, and I know without a doubt that God will do His. I can't wait to see what He has planned for my two (grown-up) babies.

I bear witness to the strength and love that God has for mothers. The Lord displays miracles in and through my children and even, dare I say, through my imperfect parenting efforts. If He will do this in my ordinary life, He will do the same for you. Thank you for joining Dineen and me for the journey we are about to share together. I pray that you are encouraged to the depths of your soul and that you experience every gift of mothering that God has stored up for you.

My friends, I don't think our parenting story ever ends. I know I still worry and pray over my son, who is now married. He and his wife are expecting my first grandchild. So it starts all over again. But this time I will get more sleep! *grin.* I will always be a mother, and I am forever thankful that God believes I am worthy of this highest and holy calling.

So are you.

Please write to me and let me know all that the Lord is doing in your life and in the lives of your children.

I love you, my friend. I really love you.

Lynn Donovan
Lynn@mismatchedandthriving.com

Dineen's Story

As I write this, I imagine you, my dear friend, sitting across from me at a coffee shop with our mugs and our hearts on the table between us. I want to tell you my story in a way that will encourage and uplift you, a fellow mom and dear sister in Jesus. I may have not met you (yet), but I love you dearly already!

Not being raised in a Christian home left many gaps in my life that, at times, have felt like setbacks as I traveled the road of motherhood. Although I dare say that in some ways it's also been an advantage, in the sense that I had only God to look to for the direction and meaning of my faith and for help as a parent. Often I felt as if I was playing catch-up as I tried to raise my kids to know Jesus. Literally as I learned and grew in my faith, they did too. That was the adventurous part. But I confess, if I could go back, knowing what I know now, there are areas in which I would have done more or would have done things differently. Probably all of us can say the same about something in our lives, but I know that God does not want us to live with regret, always looking back.

As Paul wrote to the Philippians, "Brothers and sisters, I do not consider myself yet to have taken hold of it. But one thing I do: Forgetting what is behind and straining toward what is ahead, I press on toward the goal to win the prize for which God has called me heavenward in Christ Jesus" (Phil. 3:13-14). I can't change the past (don't you wish sometimes that life had an undo button?), but each day is an opportunity to do things better than we did the day before—a huge revelation for a recovering perfectionist who would like to have learned this sooner!

God's grace and love are lavish!

I will never profess to be a perfect parent, but God has proven to me that *He* is and He is more faithful than I ever imagined. I promise you, dear reader, that I will share with you openly and authentically in the pages of this book alongside the promise that God is able to do the impossible and He more than makes up for our shortfall. Rest in that promise right now, and let its truth sink deep into your precious, mother's heart.

When people ask me to share my salvation story, I confess that I groan inwardly. I can't actually give an exact, specific moment in time at which I gave my heart to Jesus. I think that's because I continually gave it to Him from the age of four on, not out of piety but out of my great need of God's continuous presence and protection. In many ways I see myself in my youngest daughter, who seemed to have been born knowing God. I'm sure many of you reading this are nodding in agreement, either because you were this way or you have a child like this. Kids like this just get it and are often referred to as having an "old soul."

I don't know that I truly "got it," but I do know that I seemed to understand what Romans 8:28 meant before I ever read a Bible: "And we know that in all things God works for the good of those who love him, who have been called according to his purpose."

Somehow I knew that something good came out of everything bad. It just did. Now as an adult I understand that it is part of the gift of faith, which God gave to me at a very early age. Abba is ever so gentle and kind with me.

As I shared in my story in our first book, *Winning Him Without Words*, I was baptized at age four. I still remember the feel of the water on my head and the reverence I felt when I turned the parchment pages of my new Bible, even though I couldn't read a word.

I grew up an only child—a latchkey kid. I had to learn independence quickly, and I learned it well. I was raised by a single mom who loved me fiercely, and although life was less than ideal most of the time, she never let me forget that I was loved. I did have contact with my birth father growing up, but that interaction was complicated for many reasons, including what I would later find out was his mental illness. Thus I didn't have a real father figure in my life until age eleven, when my mother remarried the man I grew up calling Dad.

Even as a teenager I was driven and determined to make my life exactly what I wanted it to be. God let me walk this path for quite a while. In my teen years I dabbled with the occult, because I was hungry for the supernatural and somehow knew there was more to this life than what could be seen. However, I had no one to tell me God was more powerful than this darkness, so fear easily took root in my life.

So much of how I mothered my girls came from my examination of my childhood. You see, I had a mother who had broken familial strongholds and abuses from her childhood in her determination to keep from bringing these very issues into her daughter's life. Though she'll tell you she only did what she had to do, she is one of my greatest inspirations. She had set the pattern, and I wanted to continue improving the generations of our family.

I share all this to tell you why I walked into motherhood with that inspiration and with the *expectation* that raising my children with their dad in the picture would provide the elements that had been lacking in my childhood and translate into a much more peaceful and easy childhood for my girls. But what I didn't expect were the travails of a spiritually mis-matched home, teenage depression and a cancer diagnosis for one of my daughters, and our family dynamics having to change radically to accommodate special needs. This was the most trying time of our lives, but my daughters and I felt God draw closer to us than we ever had before.

You will find out the rest of that outcome in the first chapter, as life inevitably proves our human predictions wrong. Please know that I don't share about my difficulties to garner sympathy or pity but ultimately to show how God enters in, takes what we have to offer Him, even in our tough times, and multiplies it to meet our needs and the needs of our children. As Jesus used five loaves and two fish to feed five thousand men and many women and children, God does the same thing in our lives as mothers.

Simply said, God has our backs (see Isa. 58:8).

I say with a laugh that I've yet to meet a mother who has said, "I did a good job." We moms continually think that we fall far short of the mark, and we blame every failure in our parenting on our own lack, even when our children have reached the age of accountability. I will share with you some wise words that a dear woman said to me when my daughters were young: "You can do everything right, and in the end, your children will still make some bad choices."

God has given us free will, and He gives this same freedom to our children as well. We are called to do the best we can to raise our children to know the truth. God's truth. Then the time will come when they will have to choose whether or not they will adopt your faith and make it their own. This is said not to discourage you but to assure you that God is in control and we can trust Him. He loves your children more than you do and has a greater investment in their lives than you do. He did create them, after all.

As I write this, my daughters have just turned 19 and 23, their birthdays one week apart in the month of December. My oldest daughter just married a young man whose integrity and heart for God is greater than what I had prayed or even hoped for in my daughter's future husband.

My youngest daughter is catching up emotionally from her trials with depression and cancer, and the years she lost to depression and illness are slowly being restored. God's promises sit before her in abundance, and I pray daily for her to fully embrace them much earlier in life than her mother did.

Most importantly, I will tell you three lessons that I have found to be most valuable in life and motherhood. One, life is a journey to be enjoyed, not just endured. Every moment, every hour, every day gives us new opportunities to do things just a little better than we did the moment before. We will make mistakes, but it's what we do with those mistakes that count most in the long run.

And second, any given moment in time is simply that—a moment. It does not define our entire future—for us or for our children. So when the valley seems dark under the shadow of death, remember that what you are experiencing is just a shadow and that the sun will soon break through the darkness to lead you out of the valley and up the mountain to view God's glory. Then and only then will we gain perspective with a God's-eye view.

And finally, as the title of this book says, you are not alone. Say it with me, my precious friend: "I am not alone." God is with you every step of the way, and Lynn and I consider it a privilege and a calling to be on the path with you. We always, always, always love hearing from you! Let's take a sip of that coffee (or tea!) and share our hearts together.

Love you so very much, my dear sister in Jesus,

Dineen
Dineen@mismatchedandthriving.com

ONE

Extraordinary Kids

Trusting God to Make Up the Difference

Dineen

Are we beginning to commend ourselves again? Or do we need, like some people, letters of recommendation to you or from you? You yourselves are our letter, written on our hearts, known and read by everyone. You show that you are a letter from Christ, the result of our ministry, written not with ink but with the Spirit of the living God, not on tablets of stone but on tablets of human hearts. Such confidence we have through Christ before God. Not that we are competent in ourselves to claim anything for ourselves, but our competence comes from God. He has made us competent as ministers of a new covenant—not of the letter but of the Spirit; for the letter kills, but the Spirit gives life.

2 CORINTHIANS 3:1-6

Am I Enough?

This question has silently plagued me through the years, most certainly fueled by my insecurities and our common enemy in this world. I tell people often that I am a recovering perfectionist. It's true. As an only child of a wonderful single mom who worked two jobs at times to provide for the two of us, I had to learn to look out for myself at a very young age. It wasn't easy, but I managed. Even into adulthood I thought I had my life under control.

So when I became a mom, I thought my daughters would be so much better off with two parents than I had been with one.

My expectations were that two parents made a perfect family—and thus a life free of the struggles I'd known as a child.

Yet every time I looked at my daughters, I seemed to see everything I'd done wrong and very little I'd done right. How could my girls possibly grow up to be strong women of faith when their mother had been so late coming to the game?

Despite having two parents who loved them and who loved each other, my girls' paths to adulthood were not the perfect journeys I'd hoped for. Both of my daughters struggled with their own fears and anxieties in a world that told them they weren't good enough, weren't thin enough, just weren't enough because they didn't meet the world's one-size-fits-all expectations.

My oldest daughter, Rachel, traveled the road of middle college, because her creativity wasn't welcomed in a high school that was bent on making all its students fit one mold. And my youngest daughter, Leslie, wound up going the way of a GED after her recovery from cancer and depression.

No proms, no sweet-16 romances (maybe that was a blessing in disguise?) and no traditional high-school graduations. My girls seemed destined to walk through this life in their own unique and often pain-filled ways. The older they grew, the more I realized I had to let go of my expectations of what their lives would look like.

And especially what their faith lives would look like.

Add to that the fact that I was the spiritual leader of our family. How in the world (or should I say in the heavenly realms?) had God thought that I could raise two daughters to faith?

Even today, with my daughters now young adults, I ask myself at times, "Am I enough?" Am I enough to be the mother and friend my girls need to help them become the women God is calling them to be? How do I keep from adding my anxieties and fears to theirs and help them walk paths of victory?

And how do I help them walk paths of victory even in the choices they will make for their future? Ah, now there is a question worth exploring . . .

You Too?

Lynn and I have a wonderful, spiritually mismatched community on Facebook and on our website, and we often hear from women and men who share their concerns and prayer requests with us. As I have read these burdens and cares over the years, I have found that same question—Am I enough?—behind many of these dear people's fears. It's right there between the lines of their prayer requests, just as it is even in my own fears. But instead of leaving this question hidden within their heartfelt cares, I wanted to bring it into the open.

So I went to our Spiritually Unequal Marriage (SUM) community and asked how they would finish and then answer the question, Am I enough . . . ?

Think for a moment about how you would answer this question. These are some of the answers I received from our online community:

- Am I enough to hold the family together? To teach my kids what they need to know about God's love? To actually sanctify this house (see 1 Cor. 7:14)?
- Am I enough to teach my kids the truth of Jesus Christ and lead them to salvation? Am I enough to be a godly mom and wife, a good role model, and to help support my family emotionally and spiritually?
- Am I enough to be a mom and wife too? How do I balance both?
- Am I enough for my kids, my husband and everyone else depending on me?
- Am I enough to point the way to True North for my children and never let my flag waver no matter how fierce the storm of the world may blow—even when the storm may be my own husband?
- Am I enough to overcome my junk so I don't pass it on to my kids?
- Am I enough to overcome my own fears so my kids don't experience them firsthand?

Here's a compiled list of variations of this question: Am I enough . . .

- To do it all?
- To be Jesus to my family?
- To lead others to Christ?
- To *really* raise godly children in *this* world?
- To fulfill my God-ordained purpose on earth?
- To show my children that they need to return to the Lord?
- To be used as a vessel to provide unconditional love?

How about you, dear one? Are you asking yourself this question? Whether you're in a spiritually mismatched marriage, divorced, or a single mom, know this one truth: you aren't alone. Many women have asked the questions you are asking.

Walls, Fleeces and Unlikely Heroes

Then the LORD said to Joshua, "See, I have delivered Jericho into your hands, along with its king and its fighting men."
JOSHUA 6:2

The Bible is full of trial-filled stories about people who seemed to persevere and to overcome only by the literal grace of God. I love these huge testimonies of God's larger-than-life plans.

When Joshua and the Israelites arrived at the city of Jericho, God gave them instructions that could easily be counted ridiculous by human definition (see Josh. 6:2-7). How could marching around a wall in silence once a day for six days and marching around seven times on the seventh day bring those walls down?

But the Israelites did exactly as God instructed them. They marched around those walls once a day without making a peep for six days. Then they marched around again on that seventh day, seven times, ready to shout when the priests blew their trumpets. I read in one commentary that based upon what historians know historically and archaeologically, the front line of soldiers most likely met the tail end as the Israelites returned to camp each day.

I wish I could go back in time to see the expressions on the faces of the men who had already marched the city once as they met the eyes of the ones who had yet to go. Can you imagine what they may have said to each other? Each day's march was a test and an affirmation of their faith. They trusted God to do what they most definitely could not.

You see, these walls were the very same kind that had discouraged the spies whom Moses had sent out 40 years earlier (see Num. 13:28). Even though these marching Israelites with Joshua were from the generation after that of the spies, men who had survived the 40 years in the wilderness to see the Promised Land, I can only imagine what some of them might have been thinking:

What if we blow it like our fathers and mothers did?
What if I don't march right?
What if I don't shout loud enough?
What if I can't do this?

Whatever doubts they may have had in light of what their parents had done, they most likely kept them to themselves. I know I would have.

Then there's Gideon: "When the angel of the LORD appeared to Gideon, he said, 'The LORD is with you, mighty warrior'" (Judg. 6:12).

Have you ever read the story of Gideon? Here's this guy doing what he has to in order to appease his enemy. He spends his days and most likely his nights threshing wheat to survive, all the while hiding from a relentless enemy, the Midianites.

Then one day an angel of the Lord shows up and calls him a mighty warrior. I can see this unassuming man looking over his shoulder and doing a double take. Maybe his thoughts went something like this:

Are you talking to me?
Have you really looked at me?
I'm the smallest in my clan.
I'm thinking you want that guy over there.

You've got the wrong guy, dude!

But God is never wrong, is He? And He is, oh, so very patient. He understood Gideon's reservations and doubts and even let the man test God's calling on his life two times. A wet and a dry fleece later, Gideon prepared for battle with 32,000 men against a force nearly four times as large.

The odds still weren't looking too good, but I can picture Gideon touching the fleece that he may have tucked into his belt as a reminder of who really was the commander in charge. Maybe even God's words kept running through his fear-filled mind and heart: "I will be with you, and you will strike down all the Midianites, leaving none alive" (Judg. 6:16).

Then God told Gideon that his army was too large.

Really? Doesn't make sense in our human calculations, but God most definitely had a reason for saying it. He wanted to make sure the Israelites knew without a doubt who would be responsible for their victory. It's not that God wanted to wag His mighty finger at Gideon and say, "I told you so," but He didn't want the Israelites to forget Him—to forget that He always had their backs.

Yes, as poor Gideon stood by watching, God did the unthinkable and shrunk down Gideon's army first to 12,000 men and then to a mere 300. Can you imagine this guy looking at himself and his men and asking, "God, is this enough?"

Letting Go of Expectations and Replacing Them with God's Explanations

God has this wonderful way of showing us His truths in order to counter past failures in our lives, whether those failures were our parents' or our own, and giving us a glimpse of His amazing and failure-proof hope.

Bible stories like Joshua's and Gideon's are our stories too. We often face struggles and challenges that we know we are not capable of handling in our own strength. But when we are obedient to God's call to march around a wall, or when in our doubt we put out a fleece just to make sure God has the right person for the job, we discover God is faithful.

The walls of Jericho fell not by the hands of men but by their shouts of glory to God. One hundred and twenty thousand Midianites were defeated by 300 men, hand-picked by God, as they blew trumpets, broke jars and shouted victory for God.

Just as we ask God if we are enough for the tasks He's set before us, if we are enough to serve Him in all the areas of our lives, if we are enough to be faithful to what we know is true and to raise our children to know Him and His Son, Jesus, so too have many of God's most faithful servants asked, "Am I enough?"

The truth is, we can stop asking that question, because God has already answered it. God's explanation is, "You don't have to be enough, because I am."

Here are some more of God's explanations:

Can I do this? "For we are God's workmanship, created in Christ Jesus to do good works, which God prepared in advance for us to do" (Eph. 2:10).

How can I do this? "I can do everything through Christ, who gives me strength" (Phil. 4:13, *NLT*).

Am I alone in this? "Be still, and know that I am God" (Ps. 46:10).

Who will help me? "The LORD is my light and my salvation—whom shall I fear? The LORD is the stronghold of my life—of whom shall I be afraid?" (Ps. 27:1).

What if I fail? "No, in all these things we are more than conquerors through him who loved us" (Rom. 8:37).

What about the rough times? "And we know that in all things God works for the good of those who love him, who have been called according to his purpose" (Rom. 8:28).

I have walked with God for a long time now, and I will share with you that trusting Him for my children's future has probably been *the* most difficult challenge for me. Along with every prayer I prayed, there was a generous helping of worry.

But over the years God has proven to me over and over again that He is faithful.

He proved faithful when my husband consented to me taking my girls to church as long as I agreed that they could make their own choice about their faith when they were old enough.

God proved faithful when my oldest daughter, Rachel, read her children's Bible from cover to cover at around age 9— the first full book she'd ever read. When she accepted Jesus as her Savior at age 11. When she was horribly ostracized by her peers during a time when we were living in Europe. When God brought her through difficult stomach problems at age 16. And when God helped her let go of an unhealthy relationship and accept that she would be loved again one day by the young man God had in mind for her.

God proved faithful when my youngest daughter, Leslie, tested positive for HIV at age two after she picked up a condom in a parking lot, thinking it was a balloon. (God changed that false positive to positively negative.) He was faithful when she accepted Jesus as her Savior at age 6. When she too endured mistreatment at the hands of her peers in grade school after we moved back to the States, even to being held at knifepoint. And when at age 14 she was diagnosed with depression and later that year with a malignant brain tumor.

As I write this, my oldest daughter is 23 and just married a wonderful, godly young man who exceeds what I had hoped for and, for many years, prayed for in her future husband. Even during their engagement, they already exhibited how God created us to function as two parts of a whole in marriage. Now they are beginning their lives together as one, united before God and by their faith in Him and each other.

My youngest is now 19 and cancer free. Though she still has much to overcome, her faith (and her dog) keeps her going on the hard days. And through it all, even in the times when she was angry at God, she never stopped loving Him.

Our mother-daughter relationships are evolving into sweet friendships that allow me to not only be my girls' mom but a friend and mentor to them as well. We are growing in faith together.

One day when I came to God with my fleece and asked, "Am I enough?" He gave me this Scripture:

Such confidence we have through Christ before God. Not that we are competent in ourselves to claim anything for ourselves, *but our competence comes from God.* He has made us competent as ministers of a new covenant—not of the letter but of the Spirit; for the letter kills, but the Spirit gives life (2 Cor. 3:4-6, emphasis added).

My precious friend, drench yourself in this final piece of revelation from God's Word:

For this reason I kneel before the Father, from whom every family in heaven and on earth derives its name. I pray that out of his glorious riches he may strengthen you with power through his Spirit in your inner being, so that Christ may dwell in your hearts through faith. And I pray that you, *being rooted and established in love, may have power, together with all the Lord's holy people, to grasp how wide and long and high and deep is the love of Christ, and to know this love that surpasses knowledge—that you may be filled to the measure of all the fullness of God.*

Now to *him who is able* to do immeasurably more than all we ask or imagine, according to his power that is at work within us, to him be glory in the church and in Christ Jesus throughout all generations, for ever and ever! Amen (Eph. 3:14-21, emphasis added).

We don't have to be enough, because God is enough. And He is able, He is able, He is able!

Discovery

My dear friend, again, I wish I could talk to you in person over that cup of coffee or tea. Walk with me a little further, and take your time answering the following questions with prayerful consideration. Remember, you are not alone.

1. In hearing the answers people gave to the question, "Am I enough . . . ?" did a particular area of struggle or doubt resonate with you? How would you answer this question?

_____

_____

_____

_____

2. Besides Gideon, can you think of a biblical character who doubted whether he or she had what it took to do what God asked? Go and read that person's story now.

_____

_____

_____

_____

3. Sit in a quiet place and meet with Abba. Make a list of the doubts and fears you have about raising your kids to know Jesus. Ask God to show you a verse to counter each of your concerns. Take your time doing this, and allow God to drench you in the truth and the many promises in His Word.

_____

_____

_____

_____

4. Write down on index cards two of the Scriptures you found, and this week focus on them, memorize them and use them to pray over and for your children. Next week write down two more, and each week thereafter do the same. What changes do you see already because of doing this?

_____

_____

_____

5. What is one thing you can do on a daily basis to model your faith to your children? If your children are pre-teens, teens, or even adults, how can you be a mentor in their lives?

_____

_____

_____

6. Start a list of areas in your children's lives that you want to pray about regularly. As you work through this book, add to this list as you feel God leading you.

_____

_____

_____

Prayer

Father God, Your Word is a constant testimony to Your faithfulness. I know that You long for me to trust You not only with my life but also with the lives of my children. In reality, Lord, they belong to You. They are gifts whom You have given me to raise knowing the powerful and loving God that You are.

Lord, I ask that You equip me in every way to entrust my kids to You. And not only that, help me to truly believe You and to see Your faithfulness in our everyday lives. Help me to trust You completely with my children's futures, for the deep relationship You desire to have with my children, for the calling You are preparing for them, and for the faith journey You have uniquely designed for them.

Jesus, I want my children to know You intimately and to have vibrant relationships with You. Do whatever You need to do in their young lives to show them that You are for them 100 percent, that You love them and that You want only good for them.

Thank You, Lord, for Your amazing faithfulness. I know that You are able to do all that I have asked and more. I praise and thank You now for the ways in which You are and will be working in my children to make them effective and strong in their faith. In Your powerful and capable name, Jesus, I pray this. Amen.

Respecting Dad

Whether you are single, married, separated or divorced, Dad still has a place in the spiritual lives of your children. Remember that he is unable to understand his place in your efforts to raise your children to know Jesus. He may even be opposed to what you are doing. Continue to ask God to soften his heart toward your faith and to see its benefits to your children. If need be, plan the times you share and talk with your children about God to take place when Dad isn't present so that he won't feel threatened or feel his time with the children is impinged upon. Help your children understand that Dad's choice not to believe in God doesn't in any way mean that he doesn't love them or that he will love them less for choosing to believe in God. And help them to understand that just as God loved us so much that He sent His Son, Jesus, to save us, so too God loves their father even more than they do and wants salvation for him.

TWO

Heaven's Kids

Will My Kids Go to Heaven?

Lynn

*Train up a child in the way he should go:
and when he is old, he will not depart from it.*
PROVERBS 22:6, *KJV*

"Lord, I want a baby." I clearly remember uttering these words with an uncertain voice. As I whispered that sentence, little did I know that it would be the beginning of a miracle. At the time, three years had passed since I'd married my husband, Mike. Following our wedding he and I settled into a nice home, applied ourselves to our careers and would have been considered by anyone looking in at us a happy couple. However, we wanted a child of our own, and after nearly three years of hoping accompanied by monthly disappointment, we were yet to have a baby. Our infertility was creating a strain in our relationship. I began to blame myself for this barrenness.

It was out of my fear and pain that I whispered this desperate prayer. It was the first prayer I'd spoken since my prodigal journey had begun more than seven years earlier.

In my desperate state of mind, I finally thought about talking to the Lord. I went to my bedroom, shut the door, walked to the far side of my bed and actually kneeled to pray. I felt strange on my knees, but I finally arrived at "that place." You know, "that place" where we completely reach the end of ourselves and our self-effort. Mike and I could not conceive. And I was not able to take on the scary world of fertility treatments, since as a woman no longer in prime childbearing years, I was an unlikely candidate. Our next step, it appeared, was to give up hope and resign ourselves to the fact that we would never have a child.

Leaning on the bed, I hesitantly folded my hands and began pouring out my heart in a way I'd never prayed before. My prodigal years of wandering had taken me far away from the once-comfortable place where as a child I had spoken easily and freely to Jesus. As I prayed, tears began to brim. "Lord, I want a baby. I've been unable to have one, and I am desperate to conceive a child with my husband. Lord, will You please give me this gift? Will You please share Your kind favor and grant me a child?"

I continued to pray, but as I think back to that day, I recognize now how selfish my words were. I spoke them, however, from a true place in my heart. As I pleaded with God and laid out my reasons for asking Him for a child, I promised to recommit myself to Him. And then something began to happen.

I stopped speaking, and with my eyes closed I felt a slow, warm, tingly wave flow over me. It felt something like warm honey pouring over my head and slowly making its way down to cover the rest of my body.

A profound feeling of peace and love covered me as the wave continued. It washed gently, slowly, over me, and I felt the presence of Someone on my right side. Joy filled me. The frantic need to pray for a baby ceased in that moment. I remember smiling, a smile big and full. I opened my eyes and glanced over my shoulder. No one was there, but the peace and assurance that my prayer had been heard pervaded every pore of my body.

Now, I kid you not, all my anxiety instantly disappeared, and two weeks later a pregnancy test confirmed my deepest hope. We were pregnant.

I hesitate to share this story, because I know that many of you may have struggled with your own infertility, and God has not answered your prayers in this way. What I experienced that day while kneeling by the bed I have yet to experience again. However, if the story of my daughter's beginning isn't told in this book about parenting, I would rob the Lord of great glory and honor. It was God who answered the prayer of a young woman who scarcely had enough faith to pray.

God honored my weak faith, and over the years I have grown in my trust in the Lord through my marriage and through parenting struggles. I can tell you that God is intentional and that He uses life's difficulties to draw us closer to Him.

Nine months after my prayer, a six-pound, eleven-ounce baby girl, Caitlin Joy Donovan, arrived in our world. We call her Caitie. It was new-baby bliss. All four days of it. Then all hell broke loose in the Donovan house. (Can I say that in a Christian book?) Well, that is what it felt like.

Four days home from the hospital, and our little cherub decided that she didn't like this world. She began to fuss, cry and scream until she turned bright red and remained inconsolable. This little girl-child had developed colic. Her tiny tummy hurt all the time and specifically every afternoon and evening—from 4 P.M. to one in the morning. Out of her tiny body came ear-piercing shrieks that could have competed with the passion of a classically trained opera singer.

I paced the floor holding her. She cried. I rocked her. She cried. I bounced her. She cried louder. I looked at her and prayed. Then I cried. Then Dad took a turn. The only solace for two frazzled parents was to strap our darling baby into her vibrating bouncy chair, fasten the chair to the dryer, turn the dryer on, and then hope and pray that Caitie would feel better. She seemed to like the dryer. Go figure. Sometimes she would sleep for an hour, sometimes a little more, but the fleeting moments of peace were not nearly long enough. Then all three of us were back to walking, bouncing, crying and praying. Finally, around one A.M., exhaustion overtook the three of us, and we fell into bed, nearly comatose.

Sheesh!

God has a strange sense of humor. I remember asking myself, *Is this a test? Is God asking if we were absolutely certain that we wanted this child for whom I'd prayed?* Of course we did—minus the wailing! Thank you very much.

And then it happened. After five long months, this bois-terous infant woke up one day, and her crying had ceased. At least for the time being. Little did I know about the teen years, the hormones, and the tears that awaited us down the road. Tears are a definite part of our mothering journey. We will shed tears of joy, sadness, disappointment and elation for our children throughout their entire lives. That's who we are as a mom.

The next time I distinctly remember shedding tears over my daughter was right before we were to enroll her in kindergarten. One hot summer morning, I sat in the kitchen with my husband, sipping coffee and pondering upon our baby girl. Now five, she would start school in a few months. I had always assumed we would send our daughter to the faith-based, private school near our home, mainly because up until that point, my husband had been pleased with my decisions regarding childcare and had rarely had anything to say about my choices in the matter. I bet you know where this is going.

I spoke to my husband over my steaming cup and casually broached the subject of registering our daughter at the private school. To my complete surprise, I was broadsided by an emotionally charged and unforeseen response.

"I don't want my daughter attending private school. I want her in public school," my husband stated, flatly and firmly. Translation: "Our child is not going to a religious school."

I lowered my cup. I can assure you, my husband was staring across the table at a woman who resembled a deer in headlights. I fidgeted with the tablecloth, trying to conceal my astonishment. His words stung and hung thick in the air, purposeful and resolute.

Shaken but not down for the count, I quickly gathered my wits and set out to help him see the error of his thinking. I laid out every conceivable benefit of private school. I worked my position to convince him of the substantial value of a private education. After all, I was certain it was the best and most obvious choice of education for our girl. I conveniently omitted the spiritual element from the conversation. I saw no need to go down that path if I wanted to win this argument. My true motive, of course, was my desire to give our daughter spiritual training, but I knew that desire would rub my husband the wrong way.

My logic was flawless. I was certain he would cave to my clever and convincing reasoning.

He would have none of it.

Our conversation ended. I relented, but grudgingly, knowing it was the right thing to do for our marriage. A few days later, the Lord brought *that* verse to my attention. You know *that* verse. It can make a wife cringe:

> Wives, submit yourselves to your own husbands as you do to the Lord. For the husband is the head of the wife as Christ is the head of the church, his body, of which he is the Savior. Now as the church submits to Christ, so also wives should submit to their husbands in everything (Eph. 5:22-24).

So I let go of my desire and gave in to my husband's.

I didn't like it. Not one little bit. But the Lord truly knows what's best, and He reminded me that my obedience to His Word honors Him and opens a door for the Holy Spirit to work in my husband.

For weeks following this exchange, I couldn't shake my fear over my daughter's spiritual future. I worried, *Will she grow up to love Jesus?* For the first time I contemplated the dreaded question that all believing parents who live in a mismatched home ask: Is it possible to raise children in a home in which Daddy doesn't believe in Jesus? Would living in this home sacrifice my child's eternity?

As believers in Christ and as mothers, our thoughts and prayers for our children's eternity consume many hours. We fret over our children's future. We pray from a mother's earnest heart for our kids to know God. We beg the Lord to cement their salvation. And in the back of our minds, we are desperate to find a way to teach our kids about Christ as well as to maintain peace in our marriage. It can appear at times that this is an impossible mission.

However, over my many years of walking with the Lord, I have discovered a few truths. It *is* possible to raise kids to believe in Jesus even when Dad doesn't believe. You, as the believing parent, can help your children find and follow Jesus. These truths are trustworthy and true; you *can* raise godly children, even in a spiritually mismatched home.

Where to Start

Love the Lord your God with all your heart and with all your soul and with all your mind and with all your strength.

MARK 12:30

The most powerful thing we can do to help our children love Jesus is to love Jesus ourselves. When we love Jesus the way Mark describes in the verse above with our entire heart, soul, mind and strength, our love for Christ becomes infectious. In fact, that kind of love is ultimately irresistible.

When the love of God completely fills our hearts, it will seep out through our ordinary, daily living in subtle yet effective ways, thereby impacting our children. I have found this to be particularly true with regard to menial tasks. Cooking dinner, helping my kids with homework and driving a child to a soccer game are examples that spring to mind. Our children possess extremely watchful eyes. They perceive and analyze the adults around them. They scrutinize their parents' behavior and motives, determining if what Mom says on Sunday morning is lived out during the week. This can be a frightening thought or one that empowers.

Be empowered, my fellow mom.

Sit with the Lord daily. Pray and simply linger in the lavish love of our Savior. Pour over His holy Word. Take comfort in His promises. Out of your love relationship with God, your prayer time and your reading of His Word, your children are affected for the Kingdom. How do I know this? Because God has told us so in a very personal and powerful way in His holy Word.

Not Alone

One verse in particular gives me the greatest comfort as a mother. What is utterly fantastic about this passage is that it is written specifically for those of us who live in a spiritually mismatched home. I'm humbled and thankful to realize that God *knew* thousands of years ago that there would be marriages such as ours. What relief and freedom this truth brings to my heart. Read it with me from *THE MESSAGE* translation:

> For the rest of you who are in mixed marriages—Christian married to non-Christian—we have no explicit command from the Master. So this is what you must do. If you are a man with a wife who is not a believer but who still wants to live with you, hold on to her. If you are a woman with a husband who is not a believer but he wants to live with you, hold on to him. The unbelieving husband shares to an extent in the holiness of his wife, and the unbelieving wife is likewise touched by the holiness of her husband. Otherwise, your children would be left out; as it is, *they also are included in the spiritual purposes of God* (1 Cor. 7:12-14, *THE MESSAGE*, emphasis added).

I'm learning that when we as believers love Jesus and walk in the power and presence of the Holy Spirit, we impact our environment. And, in fact, we bring God's will and purposes into our lives and into the lives of our children. The living presence of God within us becomes so powerful that, Paul tells us, through the believing spouse every member in the home is sanctified. The living presence of God is so contagious, so powerful, that it creates an umbrella of safety over anyone who comes into that environment.

My friends, we as believers are uniquely positioned to release the purposes, the love and the very power of God into our children's lives. Our kids are then included in God's plans for their lives. They are sanctified—set apart as holy unto the Lord. They belong to the Lord. When we grasp this truth, praying with faith through the Holy Spirit for our kids, we need not live in fear for their salvation. Our love, our example, our Jesus is always enough. I believe this promise for my children's future and for their eternity.

Train Them Up

Several days following the "Kitchen Table Debacle," as I have come to call it, I sat down at a local restaurant for breakfast with a new friend. I had met Jenny the week prior at our church Bible study. She was a tad bit older than I was, and a lot wiser. She and I clicked from the start. I remember pouring out my fears about my daughter's salvation while Jenny listened. After hearing my story, she said something to me that I will never forget. She gave me a Scripture verse:

> Train up a child in the way he should go: and when he is old, he will not depart from it (Prov. 22:6, *KJV*).

Jenny looked across the table, gently holding me in her eyes. She patted my hand and said, "Lynn, you do the best you can to train your daughter and then you trust the Lord to keep His promise."

I cried.

Tears of relief. Tears of hope.

She went on to say, "The key to this verse is the word 'old.'"

Immediately I felt a wave of peace wash over me. I knew exactly what she meant. Our kids may stray from living a life for God. They might outright rebel. They might buy into the lies of the enemy and embrace the ways of the world. Or choose to discount Jesus just like Dad has done. It is a possibility. This is also true of children raised in a home with two believing parents. There are kids who choose to travel the painful path of the prodigal child. But—and how I love it that with God in the story there is always a "but"—if we have trained our children, taken advantage of every teachable moment, encouraged them to attend church (I share more on this in later chapters), and loved on them with the infectious love of Jesus, they will return to God.

I am proof of this truth!

Like Abraham, who believed God for a promise that was not fulfilled in his lifetime, we also can believe. Our child may return to his or her faith as a young adult. Or, and this is likely, their faith may resurface when they begin to have their own children. It's funny how little ones will soften a heart. Our children may not turn back to God until they are 80, when they are "old." We may never witness their running home to the Father this side of heaven, but we can trust God to hear our prayers and pleadings for them. We can take God at His word. Our hearts can rest in the security of His grace—the logic-defying, crazy, unpredictable, scandalous grace of Jesus Christ. God loves our kids with a passion and a commitment that we can't begin to understand. And that's a promise!

Never doubt that God hears our prayers for our babies, our teenagers and our ever-challenging prodigal adults. He listens when we share our concerns with Him. Our earnest prayers move Him.

Faithful and True

At the time of this writing, our daughter is nearly 18 years old and is a senior in a large public high school in Southern California. She has weathered the temptations and disappointments of teendom. She's wrangled with her faith over the past year, even struggling with anger at God at one point. Yet she will tell you that she loves Jesus, and her faith is authentic. She lives her beliefs with a courage that inspires both me and her unbelieving dad. God has walked with her every step of the way.

More than anything, as my daughter prepares to step into her next season of life on a college campus, I want her to make choices not out of guilt so as not to disappoint us, her parents, but out of her own desire to honor God. As she matures into an adult, the legacy I hope to pass along to her is a faith that is her own and a relationship with Christ that will carry her through her entire lifetime. I don't want her to make choices because they are what I want for her. I want her to make godly decisions because she is motivated out of love for our Lord. This kind of faith development takes time and effort, and the rewards are not often witnessed for years and years.

I've lived my faith and love for Jesus on purpose in front of little eyes. In the remaining chapters of this book, we will uncover what living our faith looks like to a child. But today, as my daughter approaches adulthood, I've witnessed the fruit of the years, the tears and the prayers I have uttered for her.

I was greatly encouraged recently as I witnessed my daughter's faith in action as she stood up against teen peer pressure. Several of Caitie's high-school friends invited her to attend a theatrical production that I didn't know was of questionable morality. My daughter flatly declined to attend. My heart soared when I overheard her on the phone with one of her friends, responding to the obvious questions, "Why aren't you going with us to the play?"

She said, "It just doesn't sit right with my morals. So I'm not going."

God can and will help you train up your children in the way that they should go. The best thing we can do for our kids is to love Jesus with all our heart, soul, mind and strength. Model your faith; don't preach it. Love with passion and with a giant portion of forgiveness and grace. Parent with God, and watch all that He will do, even in the home of the spiritually single.

So as I reach the end of this chapter, I can't help pondering God's amazing plans, His grace, His great love for me and my children. Many years ago, when I whispered a simple prayer as a young wife with a weak faith and asked the Lord to bless me with a child, God knew that this day would come when I would share His miracles and His wisdom as to how we can raise our children to faith in Him, even in difficult circumstances.

And now as my daughter approaches her high-school graduation, I find it interesting that once again our home is faced with an education decision. As of the writing of this chapter, my daughter has applied to a handful of colleges. Several of the universities are liberal in tone and reputation, including the University of California at Berkeley, my husband's alma mater. She has also sent several applications to Christian universities. It's utterly fascinating to me that all these years later, once again our daughter's education is a matter of stark difference of perspective in our home. However, this time I'm not fearful. I have trusted God all these years to guide my daughter. I have prayed for hours and hours over her life. And I know she is outrageously loved by God.

I think about my daughter's future frequently in this season as she considers her choice for college. And this time, the choice is completely hers.

God's love for our children is unfathomable. He is relentless in His pursuit of our kids' hearts, and He will give them every opportunity to choose life, to choose Him. We need only be the best mom we can be and then simply trust our Lord, because He will not fail to do His part.

Discovery

Mom, allow me to affirm you today. As a mother, you have a high and holy calling, with a mission to impact your children's souls. Take a moment and ask God to meet you here in these questions, to bring you affirmation, resolution and encouragement. Remember, Mom, there's no way to be a perfect mother, and a million ways to be a great one.

1. Think about the birth of each of your children. Recall the day that each one arrived. Now thank God for each of your children. Write down their names and then write out prayers of thanks. Then, next to each child's name, write out the hopes you have for that kid's faith, relationships and future.

_____

_____

_____

_____

2. How have you intentionally modeled your faith to your children?

_____

_____

_____

3. What Scripture verses bring you comfort and encouragement in your parenting?

_____

_____

_____

4. This week take five minutes every day to stop and enrich your personal relationship with Jesus. Pray, asking the Lord to lavish His love upon you and to help you become a child who receives the love of her Father.

_____

_____

_____

5. What is one thing you want to start doing to grow in your relationship with Jesus?

_____

_____

_____

6. In your daily living, how does your love for Jesus impact your children?

_____

_____

_____

7. This week make a commitment to pray daily for each of your children by name. Determine to discover one area in which each child is struggling, and commit to pray for a breakthrough in that area. Write out this prayer.

_____

_____

_____

Prayer

O Lord, fill me this hour with a fresh fire and anointing of Your love. Fill me with Your Holy Spirit so that when I'm in a room, the environment is changed by Your presence. Let Your presence impact my children for Your kingdom. Father, place in me a love for Your Son that is so full that my children desire that same kind of love with all their hearts.

Fill me with Your promises—promises that I can lean on when I'm uncertain or fearful for my kids. Help me to pray for each child by name daily and to bring them before Your throne of grace, seeking Your favor and protection for them.

Mostly, Lord, help me to be filled with grace, overflowing with compassion and kindness. Shape everything I do with forgiveness and hope. Let me love my children, guide them faithfully and remember always that they are Yours, in the name of Jesus. Amen.

Respecting Dad

This chapter focused on the truth that our personal love relationship with Christ impacts our children. This powerful concept from 1 Corinthians absolutely applies to dads as well. We as the believing mother bring God's power and love to bear in Dad's life as we simply live out our faith. Living our beliefs through everyday issues, being intentional about not preaching, and allowing our actions to do the talking are among the most respectful ways to model our faith to our children and to their father. In addition, when we do this, we teach a concept that will be extremely beneficial to the relationships our children will form as adults.

THREE

Equipped Kids

Teaching Kids the Power of Prayer and the Strength of the Sword

Lynn

Bring them up in the training and instruction of the Lord.
EPHESIANS 6:4

I am all about the practical. Give me an idea or a suggestion on how to inspire my kids to grow in their faith, and I will run with it. This chapter is full of practical ideas about how to do just that. As I sat down to write, however, the Lord whispered in my ears, "It's always about relationship."

If you remember, I grew up in church. I learned how to pray. I knew the Bible stories and all the hand motions to the songs we sang in Sunday School. But my little-girl faith wilted in my early adult years because I had Jesus in my head but not in my heart. The relationship was missing.

Leading, shaping and teaching our children begins with the practical, but it must always point to a relationship with the living God of the universe, His Son, Jesus, and the Holy Spirit. Our children will learn to love God's Word because we love God's Word. They will pray because we believe in prayer. And when you throw in some fun and a ton of laughter on this training journey, your kids will enter into an authentic love relationship with Jesus that will last a lifetime.

Who Is a Spiritual Leader?

Our online community at www.spirituallyunequalmarriage.
com often tackles many of the unique and challenging areas of
living in a spiritually mismatched union. One of the common
struggles we face has to do with spiritual leadership.

The spiritual direction of our home is monumentally important. We all wrestle with how to handle this issue well. In
my own marriage this was an area of great confusion for me.
Many difficult questions troubled my mind, such as:

- Do I wait for my husband to become a believer before
  setting the tone in our home for prayer and Bible
  reading?
- If I take any initiative to teach my kids about faith, will
  my actions be perceived as disrespecting my husband?
- Can I be the spiritual leader of our home and yet follow
  my husband's lead in other areas of our marriage?
- Will my kids listen to me if I'm not the head of the
  household?
- Does leading spiritually make me the head of the
  household?
- Am I up to the task of spiritual leadership all on my own?

Tell me that I haven't been alone in this! If you, like I have
been, are in the midst of this kind of confusion, today I want
to set your feet on a path to freedom.

Many years ago I heard this statement:

If your husband is unwilling to lead spiritually or has
abdicated his position as the spiritual leader of your
home, then God expects you, the believing wife, to step
into this role.

Upon hearing this single sentence, I felt the cloud of
confusion lift from my soul, and freedom flooded my heart. I
will add that if you are raising children as a single parent, God
looks to you to step into this role as well. Somehow I guess

I needed permission to become the leader for my kids, and it came with those words. What a relief. But how do we step into this role and do it well?

It begins with our motives. The effectiveness of our parenting and the successful navigation of our marriage greatly increase when we consistently check our motives. I had to ask myself, "Does my desire for my husband to lead our home come from a place that is me-centered or Christ-centered?"

Let me be specific. Here are some of my thoughts from years past:

- *If only he would believe, he would help me get the kids ready for church.*
- *My life would be so much easier if only he was a believer.*
- *If he believed, I wouldn't have to sit with each of the children tonight and pray with them. I wish he'd help.*
- *Going to church alone is so embarrassing.*

Okay, I know I'm not the only one to have had these kinds of thoughts. But there comes a time when we must move past ourselves and truly focus on what is Christlike. Motives born out of love and humility will move us to wake the kids on Sunday morning and take them to church, even if we must do it alone. Out of a loving heart, you can say to your husband, "Sweetie, watch the television without me for an hour. I'm going to go tuck the kids into bed and say bedtime prayers."

There are many ways you can build respect for your man and still quietly lead your family closer to Christ. More than anything, I go back to the truth of 1 Peter 3:1: win them over without words. Win your kids, your husband, your friends, your neighbor and a world that is lost and broken. Win them over with your boundless, crazy, passionate, fervent, zealous and adoring love for Jesus. When you love Jesus with all your heart, soul, mind and strength, over time it is irresistible to people. And that's a promise.

Jesus modeled humble leadership. Doing what He did is the key to leading your children when Dad doesn't believe. A happy marriage, whether it's comprised of a believing husband and wife or only a believing wife, begins with love and respect. When we make Jesus our center, then add to that a sense of humor, sprinkles of grace and heaps of forgiveness, we have a winning combination that will gently lead our children to faith.

Teachable Moments

Tiny hands clutched the plastic egg. My daughter turned her six-year-old face up at me, her eyes filled with anticipation. What would she find inside this Easter egg? She turned her attention back to the blue egg. Gently she separated the halves, only to discover that the egg was empty. Her surprised face looked up at me again, this time waiting for my explanation. "Caitie," I said, "the last egg is empty. This egg represents the empty tomb. It's empty because on Easter morning Jesus rose from the dead. Jesus is alive."

Every year since my daughter was small, I've pulled down the bin of Easter decorations from the closet, and together she and I have searched for the Resurrection Eggs.®[1] We open up the egg carton to 12 brightly colored plastic eggs that contain symbols of the Resurrection story. Opening the first egg reveals a simple donkey. And thus we share the story of Jesus entering Jerusalem on a donkey's colt. Each successive egg contains another symbol of the Passion Week, which we animate as we talk, leading us to the last egg: the empty tomb. This is one of my daughter's all-time favorite holiday traditions. Even as a teen she still loves to open the eggs and walk through the story of Easter.

This simple carton of eggs provided a profound teachable moment.

Teachable moments come in all shapes and sizes and can be age appropriate, impactful, funny and so often life-changing. These moments with our children can be created with intention, and some are spontaneous, catchable moments. As the believing parent in our home, I discovered a few creative ways to share biblical truths with my kids as well as to keep the peace with my unbelieving husband. These took the form of purposed moments in which I told the stories of Noah and the ark, Moses and the burning bush, the Good Samaritan, and the many fantastic stories about Jesus. It's my prayer that my kids will carry these stories in their hearts forever.

Teachable moments can be purposely created, but I've found that some of the most impactful and powerful opportunities to impart my faith to my kids often arrive quite by accident. They come about when we least expect them and usually arrive at the least convenient times. They occur in moments when I may be supervising several pots on the stove, rushing to get dinner on the table, and haven't one minute to spare. Yet that is the exact minute my young daughter might walk into the kitchen and ask me an unexpected question such as, "Why doesn't Dad believe?" Yikes. That's a *big* question, but it's in that precise moment that my daughter is open to discussion. I have only an instant to pour truth into her in a meaningful way, because attention spans fade quickly and kids zone out fast. What are we moms to do?

In those scenarios, stop what you are doing. Get on your kids' level and whisper a quick prayer under your breath, "Jesus, help me to say the right thing here." Then speak honestly and gently into your children's lives. "Dad isn't quite ready yet. He's still trying to figure out who Jesus is. But I believe he will figure it out, and until that day you and I just need to pray for your daddy to know Jesus. Can we do that?" I smile at her. My answer assures her, and it also encourages her to pray for her dad.

As I remember back, many teachable moments sprang up for me in all kinds of crazy places and at inconvenient times. One place in particular where we talked more about God than we did in church was in the car. Or, more aptly named, the prayermobile. I think our prayermobile came into being during my daughter's middle-school years. Middle school is a challenging time for most adolescents, and it was a difficult time for my girl as well. On any given school morning, she and I would jump in the car and head off to school. As we zipped up the street, I could see anxiety rise on my daughter's face as she contemplated the difficulties and challenges she knew she would likely face that day. My heart was moved, and spontaneously I began to pray for her as we drove. I would reach my hand over to the passenger seat and rest my hand on her knee and then quickly pray over her day. These automobile prayers went something like this:

> *Lord, today let my girl have a great day. Give her something to laugh about, let her be a good friend, and help her to remember her lessons and do well on the science test. Mostly, walk with her every minute of the day and protect her. Help her to remember that You are with her, and when she feels scared or anxious, remind her to say a quick prayer to ask for Your help. In Jesus' name. Amen.*

I would say, "Amen"; she would echo, "Amen." She would look at me, I at her, and we would smile.

All was right with the world.

These simple prayers brought Caitie peace. They modeled prayer in everyday living, and they built her faith.

Today my daughter drives to school, so I make it a point to sit with her when she arrives home, usually late in the evening after a play rehearsal. I ask about her school day. She recounts some of the hilarity of her friends' antics at lunch, then she shares her frustration with teachers or the pain of a friendship difficulty. I listen with compassion, and when she is finished getting it all out, I pray a silent and quick prayer, "Help me, Jesus, to say the right thing here." Then I casually help her regain perspective. Mostly I try to shed a ray of hope on her troubles. I don't spout off, "Well, the Bible says . . ." No, I share how her pain is understandable and how Jesus might look at the situation. What would He say about a friend who had betrayed Him?

Decide today to be ready to stop what you are doing when these kind of moments arrive and to give your kids the truth. Our kids really want to know the hard truth. They honestly desire to understand more about their faith. They want to know if Jesus can really make a difference in their crazy and mixed-message world. They want to make our faith their faith, but they have questions and need to know the *why* of it all. I frequently ask the Lord to make me keenly aware of and ready for these moments when they arrive.

These often quirky and unexpected encounters with our kids pass in an instant, but they are profound moments that stick. My daughter will always have our prayermobile conversations stored in her heart. They will guide her through her entire adult life. It's an amazing privilege to share Jesus with your child in this way.

Everyday Faith

As a believing mom, I want my kids to be guided by God's truth. When my children are adults and thrown into circumstances of uncertainty, or when they face a moral dilemma, that's precisely when all the years of sharing Bible verses with them will truly pay off. Even if they don't remember verses word for word, the basic underlying truth of God's Word will remain with them. They will have hidden God's truth in their hearts, and it will rise within them to guide them to wise and godly decisions.

Make a game of memorizing Scripture verses with your children. Offer a prize or reward for their effort. Spend time sharing Bible stories, and sing songs full of Scripture. There are a thousand and one ways to bring God's Word into your home.

Recently I asked some of our readers how they shared the Bible and prayer with their kids. They are ordinary moms just like us who are living out their faith in front of their kids' everwatchful eyes. I asked them this question: "When and how have you captured a teachable moment with one or all of your children." Here are just a few of their responses:

These moments are daily. My children see me with my Bible; they know I get up early to have quiet time. I read a devotion with them daily called *Jesus Calling* by Sarah Young. I also encourage them to pray out loud with me. Everyone gets a turn, and our prayer time continues as the requests or prayers pop into our minds. We call these "popcorn prayers."

I also drive my kids and the little neighbor girl across the street to school every morning. This little girl does not attend church and knows nothing about Christ.

For the last year and a half, she has been subjected to my kids and me putting on the Lord's armor in the car on the way to school. She now knows that as soon as we leave the house, we put on our armor to start off our day, and she puts her armor on too. It's the children (and adults) we least expect who are watching and learning from us. I praise God for this time in the morning with this little girl and my kids. —Debra

We started at an early age having devotions geared to their age level. When they were small, we read Bible stories at night together. As they grew older, the devotions were usually read while sitting at the breakfast table before they went off to school for the day. —Martha

I read a short story from a children's Bible, and we sing a praise song or hymn each night at bedtime. "Jesus Loves Me" has become a favorite. Because they are very young, I sometimes use figurines and toys to act out Bible stories—it's simple, but it really holds their attention and makes the story come to life for them—and for me. —Gillian

It's never too late to impact your kids with God's Word and with prayer. Ask God to open up opportunities, and then jump in. For more ideas from everyday, ordinary moms who are sharing their faith with the next generation, visit our ministry site, www.mismatchedandthriving.com.

Discovery

We have opportunities every day to share our faith with our children. I've found this part of parenting to be a rich adventure. I'm often surprised and delighted by the Lord as He arranges a spontaneous moment for me to share His love or a truth and His holy Word with my family. Join me now, and let's come up with a few more ideas on how to share prayer and the Bible with our kids.

1. As a mom, how do you model to your kids prayer and Bible reading as part of your relationship with God? How are you intentional in this area?

_____

_____

_____

_____

2. Is it possible to be the spiritual leader of your home and also to honor your husband as the leader in other areas? What does that look like in your daily life? Consider whether you need to make some changes in this area of your marriage relationship.

_____

_____

_____

_____

3. Look up Deuteronomy 6:6-7. How does this passage inspire you today? What would living out this passage on an everyday basis look like?

_____

_____

_____

_____

4. Describe an effective intentional moment in which you purposefully shared your faith, the Bible or prayer with your child/children?

_____

_____

_____

5. Describe a catchable moment. How did it arise, and how did you respond to it?

_____

_____

_____

6. Describe a moment that you missed. Pray now, and ask the Lord to make you keenly aware of these kinds of moments in the future.

_____

_____

_____

7. Write down (or share) a few ideas for creating intentional moments that you would like to implement in your home.

_____

_____

_____

Prayer

O Father, may all I do when sharing my faith with my children be centered in a relationship with You. Allow my children to find me reading my Bible, and let them catch me on my knees in prayer. Help me to share Your wisdom from Your holy Word and to give them the ability to use their sword to fight for justice, for love and for Your kingdom. I ask, Father, that prayer would be my children's first thought in the morning, that my children would talk with You throughout their day, and that they would end every night in conversation with You. Lord, it's this kind of relationship that will prosper them throughout their entire lives.

Lord, from this day forward make me keenly aware of teachable moments when they arrive. In those precious minutes I ask that You speak Your truth through me in a way that impacts my children for their good and Your glory. Create in our home a place where the Bible is treasured and read. Lord, let our prayers move Your heart, and lead us to live a life in Your presence.

Lord, I ask that through the years I have of sharing the Bible and praying with my kids, You will help me make it a grand adventure for them. Let my kids and me marvel at Your Word as it comes to life, and let answered prayer be commonplace in our home. Let the practical living of faith be so second nature that it lasts a lifetime. Finally, Lord, let my children's faith become the faith of their children. May the prayers and efforts of this ordinary mom be of lasting consequence for generations to come. I ask all these things in the name of Your Son, Jesus. Amen.

Respecting Dad

Sharing the Bible and praying can become a tricky matter if Dad objects to our faith or is even hostile to it. However, carving out moments with our kids that don't directly confront Dad can be easily achieved. Deuteronomy 6:6-7 tells us to share God's precepts with our children when we sit at home and when we walk along the road, when we lie down and when we get up. I think that is all we need do. Just talk about God's Word as it comes up in daily living, whether you're sitting at home or traveling in the car. Model prayer and Bible reading in the morning and before bedtime. This kind of living out your faith in front of little eyes is powerful, and it's respectful of Dad.

I also believe that the prayers of little ones asking for Daddy to know Jesus are greatly honored in heaven. The faith of a child can move mountains.

Note

1. Resurrection Eggs can be purchased through the ministry of Family Life at www.familylife.com.

FOUR

Churched Kids

Yes Church, No Church,
We All Don't Want to Go to Church

Lynn

*And let us consider how we may spur one another on toward
love and good deeds, not giving up meeting together, as some
are in the habit of doing, but encouraging one another—
and all the more as you see the Day approaching.*

HEBREWS 10:24-25

Woo-hoo! It's Sunday morning!

Opening my eyes early on a Sunday morning after a night's
rest often brings a smile to my face. My soul fills with excitement,
or perhaps even relief, knowing that I will find myself seated
in church that day. For me, worship and fellowship with my
church community was and still is a lifeline. In the early years
of my marriage, I frequently felt alone in my faith. Therefore,
Sunday morning church became critical to my spirit. I walked
into the worship center, and my soul recharged just from
knowing that I was surrounded by like-minded people who
love God.

But getting to church was often quite another story.
Shrugging on my robe on any given Sunday morning, I would
leave my sleeping husband in bed and shuffle to the coffee
pot in the kitchen. As I watched the coffee brewing, this tired

feeling of dread would begin to rise up inside. That's when my woo-hoo-it's-Sunday-morning happy face quickly turned into a boo-hoo-it's-Sunday-morning frown.

As much as I loved going to church, I hated the conflict that came with it. I can't count the number of times I've had a fight with my husband or my children or all of them on a Sunday morning while the kids and I dressed for church. Standing in the bathroom applying makeup, my husband would enter and make some offhand comment that would make me angry. That added to my negative emotions, because I was annoyed that he wouldn't be joining the family at church. Furthering the stress of the morning, the many tasks of feeding, dressing and making my kids ready for church piled onto my back. It was entirely up to me to get the kids in the car and delivered to their Sunday School classes without help from anyone—and by "anyone" I meant my stay-at-home husband. Grrrrr.

Many a Sunday I stepped into the worship center, and I wasn't smiling. And my emotions made a further twist when I glimpsed my friends seated with their spouses and children. I would entertain thoughts of envy. I pined for my family to be in church together. I longed for my family to look like my friends' families. I was desperate to fit in like a "normal" family.

Grace, Grace and More Grace

I'm fairly certain that most of us have lived through the above scenario. We simply desire to arrive at church without facing conflict at home. We are desperate to raise our children in a believer's community, and we long to fit in and look like other families at church. I know that I yearned for this kind of life for a good number of years. And there were days as I watched the coffee brewing that I would contemplate two questions: Does church really matter? And is all this worth it?

My friends, the answer to both questions is a resounding YES. But when we are living in the pain of the moment, looking conflict straight in the face and feeling the enormity of feeding, dressing and chasing two or more little ones around just to get them to church, we feel defeated.

After far too many disappointments, I'd had enough of the enemy reaching into my Sunday mornings, and I decided that I would not live frustrated any longer. The first thing I wrestled with in order to release freedom upon my Sundays was to realize that my family would not look like other families at church. And you know what? That's okay. In fact, now that I've walked this mismatched road for more than 20 years, I've come to realize that not only is it okay that I look different from my friends at church but that my oddity is in fact a unique blessing.

When I surrendered my insecurity over appearing different and also released my expectations to fit into what I believed was the "normal family design," I discovered that there were actually many of us "oddballs" in the church community. I began to notice and then come to love those who also live on the fringe of a church congregation. I saw people such as single moms, elderly women sitting alone, guys who wore shirts with martini glasses printed on them, and many who were broken and needing acceptance without judgment. I began to notice the outsiders.

Compelled by our odd commonality, I made an effort to sit next to these kinds of people so that we weren't all sitting alone. I'd gently start conversations that at times became divine encounters. I experienced the joy of reaching someone with love. My friends, we who are mismatched are the chosen who view church life from a unique perspective, often as outsiders. And just as Jesus was a church outsider, you and I are among great company and have so much to offer people— and so do our children.

Let's embrace what we are and not dwell on what we are not. Our families will look different from other churched families. That's okay. In fact, it's better than okay. It's providence. And I promise that our weekly struggle to get our kids into a community of believers is worth every effort.

Lynn Donovan and Dineen Miller

Sunday Morning Church Begins on Saturday Night

For me a triumphant Sunday morning actually began Saturday night. Determined to end the cycle of anger and disappointment with my unbeliever, I took a few strategic steps.

For starters I laid out the kids' clothes on Saturday evening. I made sure there was gas in the car, and I had a bag of snacks ready. A little reward on the way to Sunday School never hurt anybody! Sunday mornings became much easier for us with just a tiny bit of preparation. I also began to pray for Sunday morning on the night before. Right before bed I prayed something like this:

> Lord, cover our home with peace tomorrow. Place in my children an excitement for Your house and love for Your people. I ask You to place in me a spirit of calmness and patience. Place a peacefulness over my husband as well, Lord. Don't allow me to become angry and disappointed. Keep me from comparing my family to friends at church, and make me ever mindful of the fantastic and unique blessings that our family receives through Your gifts of abundance. Lord, give me energy and enthusiasm to cheerfully get my kids ready for church. Help me to breathe the Holy Spirit into them and to love them with the love of Jesus. Make tomorrow a beautiful day, and let me worship in Your house. Fill my spirit with a fresh fire and a holy anointing to walk out my faith in the coming week, in Jesus' name. Amen.

Often after church I would take my daughter shopping. She always looked forward to church and to whatever adventure I had in store for the afternoon. These days we frequently met my husband at a local restaurant for lunch.

We moms were made for community, and our kids need community too. Make every effort to encourage your kids to participate in youth group and youth activities. Save money so they can attend youth camp every year. Let's be the mother who drives our kids and their friends to midweek youth gatherings.

Since making a few adjustments on Saturday evenings, Sundays are now my favorite day of the week—every week. And I wake with joy and expectation wearing my woo-hoo-it's-Sunday-morning smile with great joy! So can you.

When Dad Objects

Over the many years that I've served in this ministry for the spiritually mismatched, I've come to find that in general, men aren't averse to their children attending church. In most marriages husbands appreciate the idea that their kids receive moral training. This is normally true as long as Dad isn't expected to participate in any way. What do we do, however, my friends, when Dad protests? This is a difficult area in which to be definitive. The diverse dynamics comprising a marriage come into play in this scenario. With this understanding I share my thoughts on handling conflict with a spouse who is opposed to the kids attending church.

I will be blunt. For me taking my kids to church is a mountain that I would die on. I hold a strong belief in the function and benefits of the body of Christ. I'm convinced, without a doubt, that our children gain much from the people of faith. They are exposed to believing adults who love Jesus. They make friends who are like-minded in faith. They gain a community that teaches morals, values and love.

As a believing mother, I am able to be an amazing example to my children every day of the week, but God created us for community and for worship. For these reasons and so many more, I would stand upon this hill with Jesus at my side and relentlessly embrace this conflict with my husband to meet somewhere in agreement about Sunday morning church attendance. I recognize that these conflicts are ugly, hurtful and can be passionate on both sides. But I'm convinced that with God and much time in prayer, traveling this road pays off.

[Jesus] said to them, "Let the children come to me. Don't stop them! For the Kingdom of God belongs to those who are like these children" (Mark 10:14, *NLT*).

Lynn Donovan and Dineen Miller

Keep your eyes focused on the eternal: salvation for our children and for our husbands. The battles can rage, but with God on our side, whom shall we fear (see Ps. 27:1)?

The Payoff

My good friend Shelly has been married for 24 years. Her son, Rickey, recently shared with me a few words about growing up in a spiritually mismatched home. Rickey is 21 years old. He says,

> I have to say that the most impacting thing that influenced my faith had to be my mother never giving me the "option" to go to church. It was mandatory. I didn't want to go, because I would look at my father staying home on a Sunday watching television or whatever else he happened to be doing, and some days that's all I wanted. However, because I was forced into that sanctuary every Sunday, I began to grow a love and desire for it. It became a necessity for me. I built relationships with the youth leaders and all the youth around me as well. Pretty soon, I was begging to go to church every opportunity I had. If there was an event at church, I made sure I was there.

I also want to share some wise words from my good friend Martha. She has raised her two children in faith. They are now ages 37 and 40 and are believers who are raising families of their own.

> My girls always loved church. I believe that was because of their Sunday School teachers, youth leaders, mission trips, church socials, etc. They all made such a huge impact on my girls. In fact, Heather, my youngest daughter, wrote a paper in college about the most influential person in her life, and it was her youth pastor. Imagine that—it wasn't me (smile).
>
> All that to say, please encourage young mothers to make the effort to take their children to church, even

when their husbands don't go. I wanted so many times to give up, especially when the kids were small. But the influence of the kind of people I mentioned above is forever planted in a child's heart. I love the song with the words, "Thank you for giving to the Lord, I am a life that was changed."

Though my kids and yours didn't have a dad who influenced them spiritually, you and I were not alone; God sent us some help. That's why I would scream from the rooftops to young mothers, "Get over yourself and go!"

Finally, I would like to share with you the words of a young woman who is now raising three little boys of her own. Heidi was raised in a spiritually mismatched home. Her mother was a believer, and her dad was not. I spoke to Heidi not long ago and asked her what it was like to grow up with parents whose faith and perspectives differed. Here is what she said:

Lynn, what profoundly stands out to me was that my mom was a true example of living out the gospel. She understood that life was all about Christ. Because she loved Jesus so much and was filled with His love, she constantly poured out that love upon me.

One of the many examples of this love that I distinctly remember from my childhood is walking home from elementary school up a long hill on a very hot day. My mother would walk to the top of the hill to meet me, and she was always holding a glass of ice water. I was teased sometimes because my mom did this, but I didn't care. I was loved. I felt loved, because no other mom did this for her child. I saw Jesus in her because she poured love out on me in a million little ways. I saw in my mother that there was never a question about her love for me and our relationship, because her love for me came out of her love for Christ. The way she loved me was the way she felt loved by God.

My mother was the manifestation of God's love for me.

Lynn, what I know to be true is that God can right any situation, even if it isn't ideal. God's love flowing through you, a believing mother, is more than enough. God fills in the empty spaces (unbelieving father). And it's beautiful.

As we draw to the end of this chapter, I realize that there may come a time when a son or daughter will reach an age at which they no longer want to attend church. The moment may be approaching when your son looks down on you because he's six foot two and still growing and says to you, "I'm not going. I'm staying home with Dad." You can't physically force your son to get in the car on a Sunday morning. His objection to church could be for many reasons, and this is where he often will gain support and permission from Dad to remain at home. How do we walk through this period and navigate it with love, grace and hope? (I share more about this in Appendix 1, "Rebellion and the Prodigal Adult.") For now, from one mom to another, be encouraged. Every effort, all the conflict and stress, all those feelings of being an oddball are worth it. A life lived for Christ is always worth the cost. Live in grace and let go of your preconceived expectations of Sunday mornings, and celebrate your nonconformist family. Dwell in the perfect grace and peace of our great God. Let His love fill in the empty spaces for you and your children.

Discovery

Mom, let this chapter encourage you as you live in the body of Christ. With all the church's imperfections, God still works miracles in and through His people. I also will ask you again to extend grace. There are Sundays when it's appropriate for you to skip church to spend time with your husband or to do things as a family. But keep Sunday morning church with the kids a consistent and high priority. As the Scriptures tell us, "Let us . . . not give up meeting together" (Heb. 10:24-25), because it's beautiful in the Lord's house.

1. Before moving further in this discovery, this is the time for you to truly contemplate and pray about your commitment to a church body. Ask yourself if you are part of a Spirit-filled church where you and your children can thrive. If you aren't sure or you are unsettled about attending church, pray and ask God for His direction and guidance in this area. Finding a church that fills your and your children's spirits takes time, effort, sometimes lots of visits and Holy Spirit-inspired prayer. Pray now if you need to. Pray every day until you are settled into a body of believers. Write your prayer.

    _____

    _____

    _____

2. Think about some of the conflict you've faced on a past Sunday morning as you prepared to leave for church. What were some of the flash points? Were they internal (disappointed expectations)? Were they with your spouse or your kids?

    _____

    _____

    _____

3. What are some actions steps you can take to manage your disappointment and your unmet expectations of yourself and others as related to church?

    _____

    _____

    _____

4. Using your answers to question number two, what can you do differently in the future to defuse conflicts with your spouse over church attendance?

_____

_____

_____

5. List action steps you can take to help your children be ready for church on Sunday mornings.

_____

_____

_____

6. What is the payoff of being in church? Describe the benefits of attending church that you recognize in your children today. What do you want for your children and their involvement in church in the future? Finally, how can you pray for your children and their church experience?

_____

_____

_____

Prayer

Heavenly Father, make me ever mindful of the need to be in Your house with my children. Lord, keep me from bitterness because I sit alone in church and must shoulder the responsibility of raising my kids in faith. Make Sunday mornings a day filled with joy in our house. Free me from disappointment and unmet expectations. Father, release into our home a hunger for us to be with other believers, and place around us Your people who model Christlikeness to my children. Let my children see Jesus in these people's faces and feel love when they are in Your house.

Father, I ask You to lead our home as we wait and pray for the salvation of my children's father. Perhaps it will be the faith of my kids who bring their father to know Christ. Help me to teach my children to hope and pray for their dad.

Help me to look for those who live on the fringe of faith and to teach my children to love those who don't fit in as well as others. Give me grace on the difficult days, energy when I'm exhausted and love that overcomes. I love You, Lord. Thank You for Your body of believers. I know that I will spend an eternity with them. Your church on earth is only a taste of the amazing friendships and love with others that we will share in heaven. In the name of my King, Jesus. Amen.

Respecting Dad

Many unbelievers' convictions about church, more specifically about religion, have been adopted over the years from misinformation and distrust. The media influence and the continuing disparaging reports regarding faith do little to dissuade negative perspectives. As we begin to understand their questions about faith and the challenges of distrust, let it encourage us to be patient with Dad and his objections to church. I believe this potentially contentious topic of church attendance can actually open the doors to discuss our faith in Jesus in a mature and calm manner. It's in these moments that we can take the focus off the negative and can accentuate the positives that come from training our children in faith. Turning our focus to virtues such as kindness, compassion, generosity and love for all people can soften a hardened heart. I know that for me, simply telling my husband, "Church makes me happy," seemed to help him come to terms with my commitment to attend church.

Church can be a difficult topic of conversation. Enter into it with love, compassion and respect. Find some point of agreement at which both you and your husband can have peace.

Finally, include Dad as much as you can and as much as he is willing in your church activities. And don't overcommit yourself to church. Many men struggle with feelings of rejection or competition due to the amount of time we spend at church. Respect and compromise are crucial. Pick and choose your battles, and cover church attendance with a ton of prayer.

FIVE

Peaceful Kids

Saying No When the World (and Dad) Says Yes

Dineen

Finally, brothers and sisters, whatever is true, whatever is noble, whatever is right, whatever is pure, whatever is lovely, whatever is admirable—if anything is excellent or praiseworthy— think about such things. Whatever you have learned or received or heard from me, or seen in me—put it into practice. And the God of peace will be with you.

PHILIPPIANS 4:8-9

My youngest daughter once told me that the more I said no to something, the more she wanted it. And she said it as if she thought I should already know and understand this!

The funny thing is, she had a point. The more we define something as off limits, the more our fallen human nature seems to want it. Diets are proof of this frustrating behavior. The most effective and long-lasting diets are those geared toward what you *can* have and include the added benefit of making permanent lifestyle changes. In other words, dump the negative connotation and spin things in a positive light. It's all about perspective.

In the writing world we call this slanting a negative point of view to a positive one. Instead of saying that something isn't valuable, it's more powerful to say it's worthless—what it *is* instead of what it *isn't*.

I have found great value in this concept, especially when relating to tweens and teens who are desperate to know what their parents are for or what they believe in, not just what they're against. Therein lies our opportunity to inspire our kids to greatness and to show them a path of righteousness worth traveling and holding to, no matter what's presented to them. As parents, we want to release the potential God has placed in our children.

The best way I know to do this is to view each person and each situation I come across as an opportunity to show Christ. To be that aroma of Jesus right in the moment (see 2 Cor. 2:14-16). In our first book, *Winning Him Without Words*, Lynn and I talked about being the aroma of Christ in our marriages. We can be this same presence in our children's lives as well. Practice what you preach, but don't preach! Lead by example. Nothing shuts a kid down faster than being subjected to a lecture. Instead of pounding at their minds, we often have to appeal to our children's hearts and engage them there first. And sometimes the best thing we can do is just listen.

It's About Legacy, Not Legalism

The promise is for you and your children and for all
who are far off—for all whom the Lord our God will call.
ACTS 2:39

In the book of Romans, Paul goes to great pains to explain that the laws the Jews had held for so long did nothing to bring them closer to God. Quite the opposite, actually. The Pharisees had turned the very laws designed to keep peace with God into the people's greatest barrier to having a relationship with Yahweh.

How you walk with God and pursue your faith on a daily basis will be your greatest influence on your children, but I can tell you from experience that most of the time you will be unaware that you are affecting anyone. You may even think you're not doing anything special at all, but you are. Whatever we make important in our lives reflects our heart to those around us. If your relationship with God comes first in your life, you will set an invaluable example to your children that will carry into their adult lives.

I remember once speaking to my oldest daughter from a place of doubt, expressing my wish that I'd done more to help her and her sister to know God better and to grow stronger in their faith. Part of that desire is like any mother's—I would rather see my children acquire the knowledge I have without having to learn the lessons painfully (I'm sure you can relate!). I can't help but wonder how much better they'd navigate the turbulent waters of the things they struggle with if I could pour what I know now into them at this stage in their young lives.

Unfortunately, that would keep my kids' faith as more an extension of mine than their own. Every child, at some point, must make the shift from living their faith under the umbrella of Mom's and claim and define it as theirs. And they too, like us, must learn what it means to have a growing relationship with God.

As I shared, I spoke to my daughter out of my doubts, but her response to me became part of my confidence in God's faithfulness: she told me that by my living out my faith every day authentically and purposefully, I'd had the most impact on her life and faith choices. Her words reminded me that God takes what we have and completes, multiplies and expands upon our offering.

We don't have to be perfect, but we do need to be intentional. Set the pattern of faith that you desire for your children—the relationship you long for them to have with their Creator—by living and pursuing it yourself. Remember too that God is partnering with you in this process, and trust that your children will walk into His plan for them in His timing. From this perspective we will witness our hopes and prayers for our children become the substance of God's plans and revelations for their lives.

Inspire Your Kids to Greatness

I have the right to do anything, you say—but not everything is beneficial. I have the right to do anything—but not everything is constructive.

1 CORINTHIANS 10:23

Lynn Donovan and Dineen Miller

My family and I moved from Memphis, Tennessee to Switzerland on the cusp of the Harry Potter craze. I was relieved in some ways to leave behind the constant barrage of debate over this book. I briefly thought I was free from dealing with the decision as to whether or not my kids would read these books—until my husband came home one day with a copy of the first volume, *The Philosopher's Stone* (the British title).

I cautioned my husband with my concerns, and after our discussion I made the decision to compromise, because I realized then that I didn't have to take a stance of defeat. Instead, I would prayerfully read the book with my oldest daughter, Rachel, and my husband so I could keep an eye on what this book shuttled into their hearts and minds. We read the book together and discovered a delightful story that we all enjoyed.

Even though my youngest daughter was too young to read it, the book gave me an open door to talk to my girls about the truth of evil in this world. What I feared would be the demise of my daughter's belief in God became an opportunity to affirm it and to share the truth that Jesus living in us makes us stronger than anything of this world.

Inevitably, as mothers we will be faced with these kinds of decisions, whether they come into our homes through a well-meaning spouse or friend, from our children's schools, or from the playmate next door. We cannot shield our kids from everything, but we can equip them to discern the truth and to discard the lies. And the sooner the better.

Ultimately, it comes back to our walk with God and to clothing ourselves in Scripture. We as mothers must be firmly grounded in the truth so we can speak from a place of understanding and authority into the lives of our children. There are times we can adapt and can guide our kids while respecting Dad, as I did with the Harry Potter books. And other times we will have to stand firm in our refusal of something, because to do otherwise would be irresponsible in regard to our children and detrimental to their future.

Media choices, books, computer games and even differing faiths—our goal as parents must always be to share views and perspectives with respect and unity. As difficult as this sounds (and it is difficult), your unbelieving spouse does have the right to share his views with your children just as you do.

One of my great challenges in being in a spiritually mismatched marriage has been to understand and accept the fact that as passionately as I believe God exists, my husband does not. Telling him that he's wrong would only bring strife and discord to our family. But as I accept what he believes and trust God to be stronger than either one of us in directing the course of our children's faith choices, many of our conflicts are made manageable.

We would like nothing better than to say to our unbelieving spouses, "Please keep your beliefs to yourself." But out of respect we must extend the same consideration to Dad that we expect for ourselves. Christ didn't judge people; He held to the truth and spoke it gently, except on those occasions when He knew a full-on confrontation was needed to oppose evil. Again, this is not easy, but it provides an opportunity for our spouse and our children to see Christ working in us.

Also, as Lynn mentioned in the previous chapter, one of our greatest challenges in walking this spiritually mismatched path is realizing that who we are and what we look like as a family will not be the same as many families we see at church. All families have similar challenges, but as wives of unbelieving husbands, our solutions will be different from those of others.

Sometimes this will bring criticism from well-intentioned fellow Christians. Remember, though, that they haven't walked in your shoes. Help these people to understand your decisions, but remain true to what you know God is leading you to do. As you are faithful to God, He will be faithful to you and to your children.

Give Your Child a Voice

In this day and age, we are faced with some frightening threats to our children. Our society urges us as parents what to teach our children for their safety. Over and over we hear what is and isn't appropriate for our kids when they are outside the home.

But what about what's *in* the home, within our child's daily world? My own childhood experience—my birth father's unpredictable nature and mental illness—made me very aware of situations my daughters could potentially walk into. But along with my concern was a desire to help my girls understand how to listen to the built-in sensitivity that God gives us through His watchful presence.

In Matthew 18, Jesus uses a child as an example of a "little one"—someone who is humble and trusting in his or her faith: "See that you do not despise one of these little ones. For I tell you that their angels in heaven always see the face of my Father in heaven" (Matt. 18:10).

I believe that our children are watched over, especially in the years between innocence and accountability. As we read the records of Jesus' time on earth, we witness Christ's affinity for children, and children's ability to recognize and love Jesus openly.

Even if your child hasn't made an active decision for Jesus yet, this little nugget in Scripture gives us rich insight into the supernatural working around our children. As Lynn shared in chapter 2 about how our faith sanctifies our family like an umbrella of protection, God does not leave our children unprotected. And our faith and prayers are part of this.

At the church I attend, I have the privilege of leading a life group. One week one of our members brought her daughter along to a meeting out of necessity. This precious eight-year-old joined us in our prayer time and boldly added her prayers to ours.

As she prayed, I gained insight into three things. One, the child spoke freely, as if speaking to a dear friend or family member. Two, she wasn't afraid to pray out loud, despite being surrounded by adults. Three, the Holy Spirit actually used her words to speak to an adult in our group about a particular area of difficulty and to give that person valuable insight.

But what struck me most was how this little girl prayed for her father, who is Muslim in faith. She spoke of her fears and concerns while affirming what she knew to be true of who she is in Jesus. She prayed openly about her discomfort in attending a mosque and her refusal to digest things her father told her that she knew to be untrue.

In other words, this little girl's mother had taught her to listen to the Holy Spirit within her and had given her a voice to express the truth even given the reality of her father's Muslim religion. I asked this amazing mom to share how she had done this:

Dineen: Kristin, when did you first realize that your daughter needed a voice to express her fears and concerns?

Kristin: I knew that there was going to be a huge spiritual battle with my husband and his belief. I prayed that God would touch our daughter's heart at a young age and build her faith each day. Thankfully, my daughter and I attended church together for the first year after I was born again, when she was three years old. This experience was a very positive one that allowed our daughter to develop a love for her Creator. She accepted the Lord at the early age of six and was baptized when she was seven. I had my doubts about her accepting the Lord at such a young age, but God was clearly doing a work in her and was answering and confirming my prayer. She was very confident about her belief and knew what it meant to accept God into her heart.

Dineen: Can you explain how you taught your daughter to express herself and still understand and respect her dad?

Kristin: Our daughter grew in the knowledge of the Bible teachings from church and the studying we did at home. I saw her heart grow and learn about our Father's love for us. It was during this time that our daughter felt the tension regarding the religious differences of her dad and I. The Lord was very careful in guiding me to pray with our daughter for our family and to respect her dad's belief. She knew in her heart that God's Word was true and living, and she knew the peace she had attending church and reading God's Word. She could see that her dad did not have the same peace in his heart, and she naturally wanted to pray for him.

Dineen: Kristin, I know this is an ongoing challenge, day to day even. How has God helped both you and your daughter navigate challenging situations?

Kristin: Through these last five years, God has been able to bring me to a place where I know and can stand on His promises for our family. He is continuing to show me daily His grace and love for our family. Through all the ups and downs we have endured over the years, God is working on my husband as well, and I am learning that praying and staying out of God's way regarding his salvation is key. My husband has very close Christian friends in his life now, and God continues to amaze me in the many ways the seeds are being planted in my husband's heart.

God's way is not our way, and I am so grateful for that! God has spoken through our daughter to me on different occasions as well, confirming her knowledge of and her relationship with the Lord. Prayer is powerful! I continue to emphasize to our daughter that she needs to keep growing closer in relationship with her Lord and Savior. She cannot have that relationship through me—it needs to be on her own time with God, and He will strengthen her through that time. I think one of the key components of our daughter's faith is seeing her mom living out her faith with her dad day to day. Especially praising and thanking God for all that He has done and continues to do in our hearts and lives!

Mom, knowing Kristin as I do, I can tell you that her heart's desire is to honor and trust God. She seeks to do this on a daily basis, and she leaves the rest to Him.

As I was out walking one day, I was listening to the song "Father of Lights" by Jesus Culture. One line especially struck me with its truth: "Love has a voice. Love has a name. Jesus. Jesus." The voice of our Shepherd is powerful and true. One of our greatest gifts to our children is to teach them to hear and to recognize Jesus' voice of love.

Give Your Child a Reason

As I shared earlier, my daughter's insight about wanting things more when we're repeatedly told that we can't have them gave me a better understanding of diplomacy. I use the word "diplomacy" intentionally, because I believe at times we are called to be diplomats in our own homes.

Honestly, this is a role I've hated for years. But God has faithfully equipped me to deal with confrontation without running to the hills in a panic. When our kids are little, it's up to us to make crucial decisions for them, but as they get older, our role slowly shifts to one of guidance. This helps our children to begin making decisions on their own.

I'm sure at times that I've given my girls more information than they needed, but out of respect for who they are (and who God has created them to be), there were times when I did this because I felt they needed the full picture to understand what was at stake. If we simply tell a child no without explaining the benefits or the costs of a decision, we lose wonderful opportunities to teach them priceless life lessons and values. Biblical values.

For example, when my youngest daughter, Leslie, was about 10, she wanted a Barbie video camera that was pretty much out of our budget. But she was determined. It showed up on her birthday and Christmas wish lists, and every time we went to the store, she bolted for the toy section to gaze at the camera longingly. Let me tell you, "no" was a tough but necessary word to keep saying.

When I was a young child, money was slim to none. I didn't ask my mother for much, because I knew we couldn't afford anything extra. So here I stood in the same place financially, but now I was playing the role of mom in the story. I wanted my daughter to understand why we couldn't buy the camera, but at the same time, I didn't want to expose her to the realities of life. I realized that I would have to explain to her the truth. So I crouched down in front of her and simply told her that putting food on the table was a higher priority than that video camera.

She didn't ask for it again after that. When she was older, my daughter told me she had never forgotten that day, because it had given her a true perspective of what really mattered.

Sometimes our kids need to accept and respect a simple no. Other times we can make saying no into an opportunity to show our kids the bigger picture of what really matters.

Give Your Child a Cause

One of my favorite people in the Bible is Paul. To a new believer Paul can come across as arrogant, but to know Paul is to realize that his confidence was completely and totally in God. Paul knew his God, and he knew that nothing was impossible through Christ (see Phil. 4:13, which happens to be my daughter Leslie's life verse).

Perhaps Paul's dramatic conversion experience gave him a leg up in the confidence area. It has taken me much longer to learn confidence than it took Paul, but what I have come to appreciate from Paul's letters is his ability to give his readers a clear understanding that all they worked for (and even what worked against them) was for a higher purpose, and it was worth all their pain and suffering.

No matter how much we may want to make our children's lives easier (I know I wanted that for my girls), we actually do our kids a disservice when we fail to help them understand that our trials are often God's tools to bring us to our full potential and calling in Him.

In raising our children to know God, we can't stop once our kids accept Jesus as their Savior. At this point our work is just beginning. But we have the Holy Spirit to partner with us in this high calling—helping our kids identify the gifts and potential God has built into them and then to use those gifts.

God's kingdom goes way beyond us. As Christian parents, we are the frontrunners of our generation, impacting lives for

God, and part of our role is to impact the next generation to do the same thing we are called to do. Even as children, God will work through our sons and daughters to impact others. I witnessed this in my daughter Leslie as she walked through her cancer journey. The way her faith helped her deal with this disease had a great effect on the social worker assigned to us by the hospital. I'll never forget how this woman thanked Leslie for showing her how important one's faith was—to the point that she started rethinking her own faith choices. After Leslie's recovery, young people who had been diagnosed with a brain tumor or cancer seemed to come her way. Even online my daughter encouraged people and gave them hope by sharing how God had helped her.

So much of what we often view as hindrances to our children's growth are ways that we can help them see God working in their lives. These things can highlight for our kids the prize God is leading them to, the strength He wants to impart to them and the wisdom they will glean for use in future situations.

Just as we teach our children the importance of a good diet and a good education, so too we must help them to see that their spiritual welfare and growth are just as crucial. This is where developing their strength of character and integrity come into play.

As David said in Psalm 101,

> I will give heed to the blameless way. When will You come to me? I will walk within my house in the integrity of my heart. I will set no worthless thing before my eyes; I hate the work of those who fall away; it shall not fasten its grip on me. A perverse heart shall depart from me; I will know no evil (vv. 2-4, *NASB*).

Even in our own homes, we will face the challenges and influences of the world, but we are not helpless. God is our partner and will give us wisdom and guidance to teach our children to live in their homes with the integrity of their hearts intact. And by this we not only impact their own young lives, but also we teach them that while in their youth they can influence their friends, their family and even their unbelieving dad for God's kingdom.

Don't Settle for Good—Settle on God

Come, my children, listen to me;
I will teach you the fear of the LORD.

PSALM 34:11

I shared in chapter 1 about the cry of our hearts, "Am I enough?" We so want to be the complete answer to our children's needs and for our challenges at home. But our greatest strength, freedom and relief come in understanding that we don't need to have all the answers. God is the most important part of our parenting equation. With Him we can do anything!

Our greatest challenge may not come in the obvious—in the clear trials and challenges in which we know what to do, pray and teach. No, our greatest challenges, I find, are the ones that present us with the choice between what's good and what's God's best. The subtle guise of the enemy can threaten our daily goal of raising our kids to know God and to have a growing relationship with Him.

We are tempted to follow the world's belief that our children must be involved in as many things as possible in order for them to become successful adults. We fill their schedules with activities like sports to keep them engaged, extra-curricular courses to make sure they excel intellectually, music lessons to ensure they're well rounded, and even extra church activities to guarantee that God's Word is getting poured into them.

These are all good things. Some of these activities will even clearly be God's best for your kids as you identify special gifts and talents in them. But don't forget to teach your children the importance of being still before God, of allowing God to break into their busy day to show them something wonderful or to remind them of a friend who needs encouragement.

As adults we fill our schedules with work and activities, and then we wonder why we are so tired and worn out. We finally come to the reality that if we want a life full of God's supernatural and full of His blessings, we need to simplify and hold our schedules loosely. Otherwise we will miss the moments in which God speaks and moves in our lives.

Teach your children this important truth now. There is nothing wrong with signing our kids up for extra activities, but don't lead them to believe they have to do it all. Teach your kids the value of selecting wisely between what is good and what is God's best for their lives. And then leave time for play and discovery, for making friends and learning the challenges of friendships, for understanding and appreciating the importance of moments in our lives to be loved and to give love to others.

Let your kids have time be still and to know God.

Let's Not Forget the Holidays

But the seed in the good soil, these are the ones who have heard the word in an honest and good heart, and hold it fast, and bear fruit with perseverance.

LUKE 8:15, *NASB*

Years ago, when my girls were around three and seven, our family spent our typical Christmas morning opening gifts, then oohing and aahing over all the pretty new things the girls had received. I recall a little later that morning sitting on the couch and feeling absolutely bereft, because nothing of our morning activities had reflected the birth of the baby Jesus. Honestly, I felt like a failure. I'd tried to incorporate the true meaning of Christmas for my children. The week before Christmas we'd made pretty little cards with the candy-cane story (how the candy cane's stripes represent the blood of Jesus and its shape is a reminder of our great Shepherd) and attached the cards to candy canes, and we then trekked through our neighborhood to hang the treats on doorknobs.

Yet there I sat, near tears, thinking Santa Claus had totally won the day. My girls didn't seem to care at all that Jesus was truly our greatest gift and the true meaning of Christmas, despite my efforts. Was I fighting a losing battle?

The truth is that our challenge comes all year long. If we wait until Christmas and Easter to teach the message of why and how Christ came and died for us, we miss our biggest opportunity to build the foundation of our Savior's life into our children's lives. We miss the chance to teach them that Christ is our greatest gift all year long.

I know sometimes it can seem hopeless, as if you're not getting through to your kids, especially if your opportunities are limited. But trust me, you are. God sees our efforts, and He adds His presence to the mix. He too wants our children to know who He is, and He's working in ways that we may not realize until we have a precious moment of revelation.

One of my daughters' favorite memories is of us baking Christmas cookies, dancing around the kitchen island and singing along to Christmas worship songs. Santa may have been on the cookies, but "Joy to the World" was ringing in my girls' ears and hearts. God has this amazing way of showing up as only He can.

On that Christmas day so long ago, as I moped to myself that my girls would never grasp that Jesus was the true heart and meaning of the day, my daughters' sweet voices lifted my head. My heart swelled as I watched their precious faces, lit with huge smiles, as they belted out "Happy Birthday."

Happy birthday to Jesus.

Discovery

Hi there, my fellow mom. I know there's a lot to think about in this chapter. But my prayer for you, even as I wrote this, was that you would not be overwhelmed but empowered! Being the spiritual leader in our homes isn't easy, I know, but you have the Creator of the universe partnering with you. And He wants your children to know Him and walk into their full potential in Christ even more than you do. Take a moment to pray for God's leading and wisdom, and then let's talk some more in the questions below. Remember, I'm rooting for you!

1. What challenges are you facing at home regarding media choices, influences in your child's life and areas in which you and Dad don't agree? Ask God to show you which things you need to take a stand for. Then ask Him to give you the words and the right timing for approaching either your spouse, your children or both in order to explain your perspective. Also ask God to prepare their hearts to hear you. Be of courage! God has your back (see Isa. 58:11).

   _____

   _____

   _____

2. Some issues seem to crop up over and over again, such as which movies your children can watch or which games they can play. My girls always complained that they were the only ones who weren't allowed to watch R-rated movies as teenagers (they later thanked me for this). Each time they griped, I reminded them of the importance of what we allowed into our minds and hearts. Is there an ongoing issue in your family about which a more detailed understanding of your perspective might help your children accept that a no answer really is for their benefit and not to punish them?

   _____

   _____

   _____

3. Consider your children's daily schedule. What seem to be the priorities in your kids' lives? Do adjustments need to be made? Pray and seek God's wisdom, and talk to your children. Talk to Dad too. Are your kids feeling stretched too thin? If so, ask them what they'd like to let go of in

order to simplify their lives. Explain to them that God wants only His best in their daily lives.

_____

_____

_____

4. Dear one, this is for you. So often when we teach our children these truths, we see things in our own lives that need a little tweaking. Is God nudging your heart over something? Have a chat with Him, and see what He wants to tell you.

_____

_____

_____

Prayer

Father God, I am so grateful for Your amazing love and faithfulness. From this moment forward I am going to trust You to help me parent my children to know these qualities about You too. I ask for supernatural strength and confidence that will reassure me on the toughest days that I'm still on the right track. I want to have an eternal Kingdom impact on the budding faith of my children so that they will know You too, Lord Jesus, and grow strong in their faith in You.

Lord Jesus, let Your presence be tangible to my children. I pray that they will know You as their friend and will run to You in their times of pain and heartache. Guard their hearts, and claim them as Yours! Let them see You working in their everyday lives. Inspire them to make good choices that honor You.

Holy Spirit, give me courage and guidance to follow Your leading as I pray for wisdom, words and strength to teach my children to make good choices. Equip me each day to walk faithfully in my calling as a mother, and show me how to rely on Your strength, Lord, and not my own. Show me the unique gifts that You have given my children, and help me lead them in how to use those gifts for Your glory. Help me to recognize the potential You have placed in my children and to inspire them to be who You created them to be.

You, Lord Jesus, are before all things, and in You all things hold together! In Your name we pray. Amen!

Respecting Dad

Keeping a "we" mentality is vital in those times when you don't agree with Dad. Whether he's in the home or has the kids on the weekends, approach him with the goal of working together with him for the good of your children. Sometimes you'll have to pick your battles prayerfully and with great care. Some are not worth fighting when you look at them against the eternal picture. Others are definitely worth fighting for. In those times trust God, and remember He's on your team. Pray for God to work in Dad's heart so that he will catch a glimpse of the importance of your perspective.

SIX

Generous Kids

Inspiring Kids to Have an "Others" Mindset

Dineen

A generous person will prosper;
whoever refreshes others will be refreshed.

PROVERBS 11:25

"Lord, help me to love others as You love them."

To this day I still remember where I was standing when I prayed this prayer for the first time. Letting God answer this prayer in me has been a process, to be sure. Some days it's easy to love everyone I meet; then other days, well—let's just say I'm not perfect. I may even blame hormones on some of those days.

But on the particular day I prayed this prayer, God showed me a picture of my heart that made me want to hide in my closet. It was definitely time for a change. Not for the people who cut me off in traffic, not for the impatient woman who kept pushing her cart into my daughter's back in the checkout line, not even for the woman at church whose compliments always felt more like cloaked barbs of criticism. Nope. I was the one who needed to change first.

The more I read the Bible and considered Jesus' compassion for everyone He met, the more I wanted to love people as He did, without judgment and definitely without fear. Caution around others is wise, but too much caution had numbed me to the needs of others.

I didn't have a clue how to change or how to love others, especially strangers, the way Jesus did. But I knew that if I prayed for help, one, God would do the loving through me, and two, He would show me how to love people. One of my favorite examples is in Mark 10 about a rich young ruler:

> As Jesus started on his way, a man ran up to him and fell on his knees before him. "Good teacher," he asked, "what must I do to inherit eternal life?"
>
> "Why do you call me good?" Jesus answered. "No one is good—except God alone. You know the commandments: 'You shall not murder, you shall not commit adultery, you shall not steal, you shall not give false testimony, you shall not defraud, honor your father and mother.'"
>
> "Teacher," he declared, "all these I have kept since I was a boy."
>
> Jesus looked at him and loved him. "One thing you lack," he said. "Go, sell everything you have and give to the poor, and you will have treasure in heaven. Then come, follow me" (Mark 10:17-21).

I love Jesus' initial reaction to the man's declaration that he's kept all the laws. Jesus looks at him first, which I believe is intended to mean that He really "sees" what is in this man's heart—the grip of wealth on his life, his priorities, maybe even his dreams—but beyond this, Jesus sees who God created him to be. I even dare to wonder if Jesus reflected back on the moment this man had been planned and created. What a thought!

And then Jesus loves him. No judgment. He sees the man's potential (who God created him to be) and his chains (attachment to wealth) all at once, and He most likely knows how the man will answer. Yet Jesus loves him unconditionally (*agape*), without conditions (no need to change first), and without expectations (no longer performance-based), before He even speaks a word to him.

Jesus saw the least of those—the lepers, the adulterous women, the demon possessed—and had great compassion for them. He not only represented but also implemented God's two greatest commandments to us—love God first and love others. That kind of love moves earth, heaven and most definitely hell.

What does Jesus see in *us* when we stand before our Savior? Even on our worst days, Jesus looks at us, truly sees us and loves us first. Flaws and all. And when we love others—the difficult to love, the ones who seem odd, and even our *children on their worst days*—we model a love that doesn't make sense to the world. We demonstrate a love that speaks volumes to our children. We show our kids what the love of Jesus looks like in action and not just on the pages of the Bible. Story becomes true to life—exactly as Jesus intended His parables to be applied.

Generosity Starts Early

Dear friends, let us love one another, for love comes from God.
1 JOHN 4:7

I have a confession to make. I grew up as an only child, which meant I never learned to share very well. Sharing is a skill I had to learn as a teenager and a young adult. Even today there are moments when the selfish monster tries to resurrect itself.

My first taste of being generous came in an anonymous gift that I gave to a homeschooling mom—the first homeschooling mom I'd ever encountered. This was before homeschooling had gained more credibility, so her schooling choice for her kids and her family's simple lifestyle made them appear different to me at the time. This woman shared during Bible study one day that she didn't have enough money to buy the educational materials she needed, and she planned to muddle through and make her own.

After listening to her story, I left the study with her burden on my heart, determined to help her without diminishing her dignity. Just as I remember the day I dared to pray that prayer to love people, I remember the day that I gleefully listened to this mom praise God for the anonymous provision for her financial need. I was the one who truly received a gift that day.

When I became a mother of two, I hadn't a clue as to the protocol and dynamics of siblings. I was totally lost! Thank goodness my husband had some experience growing up with two younger brothers.

My youngest daughter seemed to be born with a generous spirit. She'd find money all over the place, and she never wanted to keep it. Even her allowance most times wound up spent on her family or friends. At first I would try to check or control her generosity, but when I did, God checked me. He'd created this little girl to be exactly the way she was—generous and giving.

When Leslie was five years old, our family went to a student orientation at the Swiss school that our daughters would soon attend. At the time my daughter absolutely adored horses, and she loved her rainbow-colored My Little Pony that went everywhere with her. She brought her cherished toy with her that day. While her dad and I toured the school, she stayed with the younger kindergarten kids.

When the tour was finished, I went back to collect her and her pony. Only there stood Leslie with no pony. I asked her where it was. She pointed to a little girl across the room, who now had the toy in a small animal carrier. Turns out that the little girl had been inconsolable over the loss of her pet hamster (and former resident of the carrier). Leslie had seen a need and a way that she could help fill it.

I couldn't imagine my daughter being happy without her rainbow pony. I waited and watched her through the evening and at bedtime, convinced that regret would surely set in. It never did.

I learned a lot from her. I learned how to be generous with my own possessions, my love, my very heart. I learned to let go and not try to control how God moved in my daughter to do something bighearted for another.

What I witnessed most strongly in my daughter was that her giving didn't happen at her convenience or her specifications. Often what she felt led to give was something precious to her. She gave sacrificially and with a joyful heart. In those times it took great effort on my part not to interfere. My selfishness would threaten to jump in with the best of intentions. I didn't want Leslie to give away that rainbow pony that she'd slept with every night for months. But in her little but huge heart, she saw another heart that needed the pony more, and she was willing to give what meant most to her in order to help.

Sometimes generosity comes naturally to our children. Sometimes not so much. But for those kids in whom generosity is not a spontaneous action, we need only lead them by our own actions. I didn't model generosity early on to my oldest daughter (this is one of those areas, my dear reader, in which I told you at the beginning of this book that I would be utterly authentic), and I had to help my daughter along in this area when her baby sister came along. She bloomed beautifully though, and her generosity now comes in the care, thought and time she puts into a gift. She makes her gifts unique to the receiver, using her artistic talent and love. She gives a part of herself in this way. And it is precious.

Giving and generosity come in many forms—some tangible and some, very often, intangible. The key is to let the Holy Spirit be the One in control. If I can impart to you, dear friend, one important piece of wisdom, it is this: As you catch glimpses of a generous spirit in your children, be careful to let them walk in the spiritual gifts God has planned for them. God's handiwork in our kids will surprise us, because it often looks nothing like we'd expect. There are so many ways that individuals can give of their resources and our time. All of these ways are special, and when guided by God's hand, they become the substance of miracles.

Through our prayers, the Holy Spirit works to show us these gifts in our children. We can ask God to give us wisdom and guidance to help our children learn and grow in them as well. The Holy Spirit will show you how to walk this path for yourself and your children.

If you give your children an allowance, teach them that their allowance is God's provision and blessing to them through you. Give them two piggy banks, and show them how to put aside in one of them a portion for Jesus. Then give them the joy of putting that money in the offering tray or giving it to the children's ministry at church.

My home church provides a giving opportunity for our children each Sunday during the special time we have for the kids to sit up front and listen to the pastor tell them a story. These precious little ones can't wait to put their coins in the money bank (usually shaped to represent whatever they are raising money for—a sheep, a beehive, etc.) because they know their money is helping those in need. Our kids have purchased sheep and cows and beehives through World Vision and other programs.

Whether it's sharing toys, time, love—whatever your child does best—encourage your kids in this area, and help them grow into giving teenagers who will shock the world with their generosity.

My youngest daughter just celebrated her nineteenth birthday and received a Visa gift card from one of her grandmothers. We went to the drugstore one day shortly after her birthday and there ran into the homeless gentleman whom we see periodically with his cat. He's been hit with hard times, and he takes small jobs wherever he can get them.

That day as I went into the store, I didn't realize that my daughter had lagged behind me. When she caught up to me, she told me she'd stopped to say hello to our homeless friend and to give him some of her birthday money. I thought she meant five dollars or so. Turns out she gave him the Visa gift card. Mother that I am, I had to ask if she was sure about that, especially in light of her current unemployed status.

She smiled and said yes, that it made her happy. She gave him what she had, and she gave from her heart. Like the woman who gave her only two coins at the temple (see Luke 21:1-4), my daughter gave without reservation. She inspired me that day.

I hope I'll be just like her when I grow up.

Seeing the Hearts and Needs of Others

"You're familiar with the old written law, 'Love your friend,' and its unwritten companion, 'Hate your enemy.' I'm challenging that. I'm telling you to love your enemies. Let them bring out the

*best in you, not the worst. When someone gives you a hard time,
respond with the energies of prayer, for then you are working out
of your true selves, your God-created selves. This is what God does.
He gives his best—the sun to warm and the rain to nourish—to
everyone, regardless: the good and bad, the nice and nasty.*

MATTHEW 5:43-45 (*THE MESSAGE*)

"I hate him."

It pained me to hear my oldest daughter Rachel's words.
I could completely understand why she hated this boy who
seemed intent on making her life a living hell. For the first time
in my life, I too felt hatred toward another human being. And
a child to boot!

We were living in Switzerland at the time, and my girls
attended the local school in the village where we lived. It
was a small community, and the school system kept the
students in the same groups for three years at a time. That
made it very difficult for a new person to enter the picture.
Rachel's inexperience and inability to speak the local language
contributed to her exclusion from social circles at school, and
eventually she became a target.

At the time the school system was just starting to address
the issue of what they called mobbing. What we call bullying.
And my daughter was experiencing it at the worst level I'd ever
seen. One particular kid had managed to turn an entire class
against her, including her only friend. He even stalked her
when she walked home.

One day Rachel raced home in tears because two of the
boys in cahoots with this young man were following her and
trying to scare her. I went to the home of the instigator to
confront his parents. His mother opened the door, and there
this boy stood behind her, the most innocent look on his face,
saying he had no idea what was going on. I knew then that I
had a formidable pint-sized enemy. Very sobering.

I began to pray for my daughter's protection, for this young
man to stop his harassment, for God to change him or take
him and his family out of our community. But I also prayed for
wisdom and insight. What made this boy behave so horribly?

Over the next few months, God showed me. His father traveled constantly, and his mother was a severe alcoholic. As much as I wanted to hate this boy for hurting my daughter to the point of severe depression, which kept her home many days and in therapy for months, my heart broke for him.

I had to help my daughter see this too. Not to justify what had been done to her but to help her understand. Because if she could understand that this young man's life was so full of pain and empty of God that his only relief came from hurting others, she could begin to forgive her enemy and even to pray for him over time so that she could experience peace and healing over the situation.

I told my daughter how I was praying for her and over her. Then one day we found out that this boy's family was moving back to England. In that answer to prayer, my daughter saw firsthand the faithfulness of God. As did I—one of the most painful and powerful lessons in my life.

Some of the most opportune moments I've had to speak these kinds of truths to my girls have come in our car rides home from school. After-school drives provide precious time for our kids to process their day and to download valuable information to us as moms. But whatever time this kind of discussion happens in your day, pay close attention to what your children tell you, and above all, listen to them first. Sometimes what's really bothering them is what they don't say, and we have to read between the lines. Let your children speak their heart, their hurts and even their hates. Tell them that you understand, and then help them to move to places of forgiveness and generosity. First and foremost, your kids need to know that you are on their side.

Finally, lead them to pray for their enemies. Help them see beyond the nice and the nasty and to see people's hearts. These are life skills they will need the rest of their lives in order to walk into adulthood with the knowledge that first, we live in a world of broken people, and second, we stand among those ranks. But we have a Savior who came in power and love to rescue *all* of us.

He heals the brokenhearted and binds up their wounds (Ps. 147:3).

The Spirit of the Lord is on me, because he has anointed me to proclaim good news to the poor. He has sent me to proclaim freedom for the prisoners and recovery of sight for the blind, to set the oppressed free (Luke 4:18).

This teaching is the birthing place of a missions mindset. This doesn't mean that you're sending your kids to other parts of the world. It means that you're teaching them to walk daily in a Kingdom mindset, to see others and to be sensitive to what the Holy Spirit wants to show them.

Just recently I had a moment of reflection and a pang of regret. I asked my oldest daughter if she ever regretted what she went through during our time in Switzerland, which, other than her school experience, was one of the best experiences of our lives! She said no, that what happened to her then was part of who she is today. I was amazed, and I praised God again for what He had taught me during that most difficult time. And what He had obviously taught Rachel too.

Above all else, and most importantly for our children, God is faithful. Always. That's one of His greatest promises.

Discovery

My precious friend, I'll bet that you do more to model generosity to your children than you realize. When I reflected back on my daughter giving away her birthday money, I remembered that just a few weeks before, I'd given a homeless family the ten-dollar bill I had in my wallet—money I'd earned selling one of my novels. Part of me wanted some of the cash for myself, but when I saw this family, I couldn't hold back. My daughter had done the same. God has an amazing way of softening our hearts at just the right time and then taking our small offerings and turning them into rich blessings for the recipients, and especially for the giver. Walk through a few

more questions and thoughts with me. My heart is yours. I
freely give it to you.

1. Make a list of your favorite stories from the New Testament,
    then pick one that shows Jesus' heart for people, no matter
    who they are. Read that story as a bedtime story to your
    children (or at a time that suits your family time best).
    Have fun with it; act it out. Ask your kids what they think
    Jesus wanted the people in the story to learn. Then ask
    them what they think Jesus wants them to learn. Then
    read through your new list of stories in days to come!

    _____

    _____

    _____

2. I shared with you my journey to loving people. I can look
    back and see how vital this journey was for my future in
    serving others and to give me a heart for women who are
    walking similar paths to my own. How about you? Do you
    see an area in your life in which God is calling you to love
    others specifically? How can you model this for your kids?

    _____

    _____

    _____

3. One of my favorite "generosity projects" that my daughter
    and I have done together is to support a World Vision
    child. My daughter allotted part of her allowance to help
    support a little boy in Zimbabwe who is HIV positive. The
    reports we receive on this little guy give us visual proof
    that we are making a difference in his life. (At the time
    of editing this book, we found out he now knows Jesus!)

What project could you and your kids do together? Think outside the box, and don't limit your project to money. We can give of our time, our energy and our talents. One idea is to draw pictures and cards for the elderly in a nearby retirement home. What a way to bless others!

_____

_____

_____

4. Do you believe that God is faithful to you and your children? If you struggle in this area, I encourage you to pray about it. Ask God to show you times when He's been faithful to you that perhaps you have never recognized. Write these down in a journal, and continue adding to them. That way when you wonder or doubt, you can go back and read the stories. For further affirmation, read the following Scriptures, which give just a glimpse of God's faithful character: 1 Corinthians 1:9, Romans 3:3-4, Deuteronomy 7:9, Psalm 33:4 and Psalm 91:3-6.

_____

_____

_____

Prayer

Father God, thank You for Your faithfulness to me. Your Son, Jesus, is our greatest proof of that faithfulness and of Your outstanding and astonishing love. Lord Jesus, help me to love others as You love them, and help me to model this love to my children. Right now I confess any unforgiveness or bitterness that I am holding on to. I want to walk in the full freedom of Your forgiveness. When I struggle in this area, nudge my spirit to bring my hurts before You again without judgment or condemnation of others.

Holy Spirit, guide me each day to help my children live in an awareness of God's kingdom. Help me to walk in this awareness too. Help us to see those who need our love and prayers, even if it's simply someone alongside the road who has been in an accident. Show me the times when I can live and love as Jesus does right in front of my family.

And thank You, Lord Jesus, for Your great compassion! You love us to the point of death. I commit my heart to You, I entrust my children into Your most capable hands, and I choose today to believe that You are and will always be faithful to me and to my children.

In Your powerful name, Jesus. Amen.

Respecting Dad

Whatever "generosity project" you decide upon, run it by Dad first, especially if he's the one handling the family budget. If you think he might balk at the idea, think about presenting him with multiple ideas, and involve him in your decision making. Even invite him to join you. These projects don't have to be strictly church activities. There are so many causes that we can help and support these days. Research these carefully, or create one of your own. Maybe the elderly neighbor next door could benefit from a home-cooked meal once a week or needs a pet walked or the lawn mowed. Doing this will be a wonderful way for you and your children to exemplify Jesus to Dad as well.

SEVEN

Authentic Kids

"Real Deal" Faith Leads to "Real Deal" Kids

Dineen

Everyone who heard this wondered about it, asking, "What then is this child going to be?" For the Lord's hand was with him.

LUKE 1:66

From the moment we find out we're pregnant, we wonder what our child will be like. We imagine great things for our children as they begin to walk and talk. Will he be the one to find the cure for cancer? Will she one day become president? Or will he be the first to walk on Mars? (For years my oldest daughter, Rachel, claimed that she would!)

The people of Judea asked this very thing about John when his father's mouth was opened and he could once again speak (see Luke 1:64-66). Zechariah praised God and then prophesied over his son, who would be called the prophet of the Most High—Jesus. I can't even imagine what those friends and neighbors were thinking as they listened to a father prophesy such a high calling for his newborn child.

Zechariah is a great example of a parent following God's lead. He had a rough start, which resulted in the loss of his voice for the duration of his wife Elizabeth's pregnancy, but in the end, he shined as a parent. He believed in God's plan for his son, and by his words of praise, he embraced that plan.

One of the saddest things I've seen in our years living in Silicon Valley (in California) is when parents determine the paths of their children without considering what their children are gifted by God to do or, as the world says, what they are naturally prone to do. Through their kids' middle and high school years, parents make these teenagers' class choices, and their career decisions are set.

My oldest daughter, Rachel, is an amazing artist. (We joke that she was born with a pencil in her hand. Her father and I have encouraged her pursuit of this passion all her life, although we wondered during her phase of wanting to be a Mars walker . . .) When she was in high school, she raved about the artistic talent of one of her friends. I asked Rachel if her friend was in her art class. She said no, that this girl wasn't allowed to pursue her art. Her parents had already decided her future for her—to be a dental hygienist. It broke my heart as I envisioned this precious teenage girl locked into a path that had nothing to do with how God created her.

Such standards place a child's value squarely on their performance. These kids are only affirmed as long as they succeed, and when they don't, they identify themselves as failures. It's a set-up for disaster.

By teaching our children to define themselves by who they are in Jesus and not by what they do, we communicate to them that God's hand has been with them since before they were born. That's a confidence and a reassurance that will stand up for our children on any schoolyard, in the midst of peer pressure and all the way through adulthood.

Who Are They?

And I pray that you, being rooted and established in love, may have power, together with all the Lords holy people, to grasp how wide and long and high and deep is the love of Christ.
EPHESIANS 3:17-18

I love the book of Ephesians, because it's all about who we are in Christ. Paul (yes, here he is again) uses words like "accepted," "adopted," "blessed," "chosen," "forgiven," "predestined," "redeemed," "given," "loves" and "lavished." I love that last word of all, because it attempts to capture the extravagance of God's love for us. I say "attempts," because I can only think of one word that adequately depicts God's love for us.

Jesus.

When we begin to grasp how deeply we are loved by our Father God, shown in His Son's willing sacrifice on our behalf, our identity becomes rooted in that love. That's why it's so crucial that our children understand who they are in Jesus, because this is their greatest foundation and strength.

Without this truth embedded deeply in our hearts, the inevitable trials of life will bring down our world in the torrents of the storms we face.

> As for everyone who comes to me and hears my words and puts them into practice, I will show you what they are like. They are like a man building a house, who dug down deep and laid the foundation on rock. When a flood came, the torrent struck that house but could not shake it, because it was well built. But the one who hears my words and does not put them into practice is like a man who built a house on the ground without a foundation. The moment the torrent struck that house, it collapsed and its destruction was complete (Luke 6:47-49).

My dear fellow mom, please hear my next words with the intent with which I speak them, in love and in truth: you cannot teach what you don't effectively know and believe. If you are unclear as to your own identity in Christ, start learning the truth of who you are now. We've provided a wonderful list of Scriptures at the back of this book, each verse affirming the truths of who we are in Jesus. As you learn each one, share it with your children. Take your kids on this learning journey with you. Make a game of it! Speak these truths over yourself and over your children. Pray them out loud. My daughter Rachel told me recently that she learned to pray well by listening to me when I prayed. Even in our prayers at the dinner table, at bedtime, or in the car on the way to school, we can set an example and teach our children what faith looks like in action.

Knowing our identity in Christ and living out our faith authentically are the most important truths you will ever impart to your children, because when we are confident in who we are and whose we are, we are seated firmly in power and authority in Jesus. We live our faith from a solid-rock foundation that keeps us strong in the storms (trials, challenges and enemy attacks).

And that is the kind of faith we want to show our children and impart to them. If what we teach them doesn't match up with how we are living our faith, then they will see Christianity only in theory.

God as Our Confidence and Competence— and as Theirs

You show that you are a letter from Christ, the result of our ministry, written not with ink but with the Spirit of the living God, not on tablets of stone but on tablets of human hearts. Such confidence we have through Christ before God. Not that we are competent in ourselves to claim anything for ourselves, but our competence comes from God. He has made us competent as ministers of a new covenant—not of the letter but of the Spirit; for the letter kills, but the Spirit gives life.

2 CORINTHIANS 3:3-6

I know that I shared these Scriptures in chapter 1, but I want to share with you how God led me to these gems above as I entered the world of speaking. I grew more comfortable (and confident!) doing radio interviews following the release of our first book, but following that I had invitations to speak to groups. Just a few, but enough to stir up my doubts and inse-curities. You see, I'm very soft spoken. All through my school years, my teachers commended me on my academic abilities, but (yep, there's a "but") they also always pointed out my soft voice, telling me that I needed to speak up.

So there I sat one morning in prayer, telling God that maybe He had the wrong gal. I wanted to speak and share the truths He'd given me, but how could I speak to groups when people might not be able to even hear me! Simply speaking louder wasn't going to solve the issue either. I'd tried that in the past and wound up with only a sore throat and achy ears to show for it.

Then God reminded me of Moses. There was a man with a much bigger calling than I would ever have. And he had argued with God too. I didn't want to be like Moses in that way, though. I wanted to trust God and follow His lead, but I needed a little reassurance.

That's when God made it clear to me, by leading me to 2 Corinthians 3:3-6, that He was the source of my confidence and competence. And I realized that's exactly the way God intended it to be. My soft voice wouldn't hinder the message He wanted to speak to those who needed it. In fact, since then I've discovered that what I once perceived to be a weakness has become a strength through God. Many women have approached me after a speaking engagement and thanked me for my soft-spoken voice, saying that because of it they were able to really listen and follow my words.

I just shake my head in wonder. I still don't understand how God does it, but He does. He makes sure that the real message-giver is Him and not me, because my confidence is in His ability, not mine.

That's the kind of confidence that makes our faith attractive and "catchable" to everyone around us, especially to our kids. I truly believe the key to this is trust in God, because God will continually push us outside our comfort zone, and He will do this with our children as well.

There are probably times when you want to run interference for your kids and to protect them from situations at school, from conflicts with friends and from their struggles to find their way in this world. But it's in times like these that your children need to walk through their circumstances—while you teach them how to trust God in the process, show them how to pray about their challenges, and share with them from your own experiences how God has been your strength and confidence. Our stories and testimonies of God's work in our lives are our most powerful tool to encourage and strengthen those we love in our home, our church and even among our unbelieving friends.

Now imagine your children in a place of confidence in God as they walk out the door each day for school, go to a friend's house to hang out, or go off to college?

How competent does your God look now?

Instilling the Desire in Our Kids to Please God Above Others

Am I now trying to win the approval of human beings, or of God? Or am I trying to please people? If I were still trying to please people, I would not be a servant of Christ.

GALATIANS 1:10

I admit right now that I am a people pleaser in recovery. In the past, when my efforts to please those around me didn't work, I took it as a personal failure. What I finally learned, however, is that people are fickle. What makes people happy one day could very well make them miserable the next as their circumstances change.

What made this brutally clear to me, though, was when I saw the tendency to try to please people in my youngest daughter. Leslie made it her mission to make everyone happy. As a young child she did this out of joy and without expectations, but when she grew to be a teenager, and expectations regarding others' responses entered the picture, I watched my poor girl suffer disappointment after disappointment.

As God worked to change this habit in me, He gave me the wisdom, strength and courage to help my daughter too. When I see that she's frustrated over someone's reaction (or lack thereof) to a service she's performed, I remind her that when we hold high expectations of those we seek to serve, our motivation is wrongly placed. We are looking for own benefit instead of purely seeking to benefit the person we are serving. Ultimately, we are to serve others to please God.

If our desire to help and serve others stems in any way from a need of our own—to gain approval, to make someone like us, or to appear more than we are—we are destined for disappointment. We are all flawed and unpredictable people. Thankfully, however, God doesn't change, and what pleases Him is always for our benefit as well.

Here lies one of your most powerful opportunities for inspiring your children to greatness. When we hold true to what God is calling us to do, when we serve others out of our love for God and a desire to please Him and Him alone, when our heart's desire is to please God above others even in the face of criticism—even criticism in our own home—we inspire our children to rise above the world's clamor to fit in and please their peers, or even to please Dad.

Just recently my daughter Rachel faced a huge decision about her future. One path was the "expected" choice, which meant spending at least one to two more years in college (she'd already completed five) taking specialized but required courses to do illustration work she despised, despite the fact that she already had an extensive portfolio. The other path presented more opportunities for her to work right away and offered an income for her to do the type of artwork she loves and wants to pursue long term. Rachel's biggest fear lay in what her friends and professors would think of her for not finishing her degree. She didn't want to let anyone down.

We spent a tear-filled evening talking about her options and ultimately what direction she felt God was calling her to pursue in accordance with how He had designed her and her artistic talent. She made the tough call to leave college and to move into her career.

The next day I took her to a doctor's appointment, and afterward, as we hopped into the car, Rachel expressed her worry again. Just as I was about to tell her to trust God with her future (and even to remind her that Jeremiah 29:11 had been her Bible verse for that year), a vivid double rainbow appeared in the sky.

I love it when God shows off. All we have to do is look for Him. Rachel claimed that rainbow as a gift from God affirming her decision. The next several weeks proved her choice right, as door after door opened for her for work and for connections in the industry. And her peers and professors all supported her decision. One professor even told her that he was wondering when she'd finally make this choice, because it was clearly the right one for her.

These kinds of experiences have equipped my daughters with a better understanding of God's role in their lives, with knowledge of how to look for His presence and to follow His lead, and with a desire to please God over others.

My dear mom, none of us will be perfect in this area. Sometimes the line between pleasing God and pleasing others can be smudgy and gray. Trust God to help you navigate this area in your own life and in your children's lives. As I shared in chapter 5, the key to doing this is allowing God's love to work through us.

Claiming Their Faith

Don't be surprised if, as Lynn mentioned earlier, your compliant, Jesus-loving child one day becomes a questioning teenager who doesn't want to go to church anymore. For some parents this metamorphosis never comes, and their teenagers enter into adulthood with their faith intact. But for others of us (yes, I'm with you others), this change just shows up one Sunday morning, and we're left wondering what happened overnight.

Actually, this is pretty normal. Does that make you feel any better? I pray that it does, but let me encourage you to keep praying for your teenager as they push and pull at what has been defined in the home until now as Mom's faith. At some point our children need to move away from defining their faith by Mom's and to claim it as their own.

This can be a tumultuous time full of worry and nagging, or it can be a time for us as moms to trust God and to know that He's definitely in the mix. In these transitions, God will show up and surprise us in the most amazing ways.

When my daughter Leslie went through her second phase of brain surgery, she asked to see the movie *Oliver & Company*, a cartoon film that she remembered and loved from her younger years. I don't know what made her suddenly want to see this movie again, but I was determined to find it for her. I knew the movie would be a comfort to Leslie, because she's such an animal lover, and this film exceeded the cuteness factor in that category. What better way to get her mind off her brain (yes, pun intended)?

I started with the usual online retail sources, only to discover that the move was at that time locked up tight in the Disney vault. A nurse told me the hospital (Lucile Packard Children's Hospital) had a movie library. I called the library's number, left a message and prayed. A couple hours later I received a call back. They didn't have a copy in their library. I prayed again, then called a friend I suspected might just have a copy. Turned out she didn't, but our other friend did. They would make the 45-minute trip to the hospital together the next day to visit and to make it possible for Leslie to watch the movie when the hospital staff moved her from PICU to a room. Prayer answered!

The next evening my friend walked into the room and handed me the DVD. I reached up to turn on the VHS/DVD combo player in the room and noticed a tape was already in it. I hit eject.

Oliver & Company popped out.

I kid you not. I turned around holding the tape in one hand and the DVD in the other, mouth hanging open in shock. I couldn't believe it. Neither could my friends.

Leslie laughed and later shared with me that this made her feel like God was watching out for her.

A while back, my oldest daughter was struggling a bit financially right after starting college (aren't all college students?). She found a nice chair at a yard sale for $20. Some time later, she found $20.25 wedged in the frame under the cushion! As she told me the story, I pointed out that God had provided for her not just the money for the chair but a little extra too.

Mom, don't be afraid to point out these God moments to your kids so they can learn to use their spiritual antennae.

I once heard a pastor say jokingly that if you want to see
something get done, ask a new believer to pray for it. He had
a point, I dare say. Those who are new believers just stepping
into faith seem to experience more answered prayer than us
long-time believers. I personally believe that God takes special
care of those who are in delicate places in their faith, including
our teenagers. Through that event in the hospital and through
many others, God has made His presence known to my
daughters, big time. Today they have no doubts whatsoever
as to God's presence in their lives. That doesn't mean they're
always on track, but even when they're not, they know exactly
where to find God.

We help our children stand strongest in their faith and
values when we set an example for them and teach them to
look for God's presence in their lives. Even when my girls were
little, some of my best teaching times with them came as we
explored nature and talked about God's amazing creation,
which included them. With God's strength and help, we can
be strong in our own faith and be the launching point for our
kids to break free from us and sail the waters of their own faith
with confidence and freedom.

Discovery

My friend, I hope you're feeling more and more empowered
as you've worked through each chapter and answered the
study questions. I'm praying for that. Even as I asked God
for the words for this chapter, I prayed that you would find
encouragement and strength in the stories I've shared with you.
You're more than halfway through the book now. Just walk
with us a little further, and let us love on you a while longer.
God has all your concerns in His most capable hands. You can
trust that fact for yourself and for your beautiful children.

1. When you think about your children's future, what do you
    imagine for them? Pray and ask God to show you what gifts
    and talents He's placed in them. Start a journal for your
    kids (maybe even a separate one for each child) so that you

can write these down along with additional insights that God will give you as your children grow.

_____

_____

_____

2. Every January I ask God for a specific Scripture to pray for each of my daughters throughout the year. I love sharing these with them. Ask God for specific Scriptures and issues to pray over for your children. Be sure to write these down too in the journal you started.

_____

_____

_____

3. I mentioned earlier in this chapter the list of Scriptures in the back of this book. Use this index, "My Identity in Christ," to help you and your children understand who each of you are in Jesus. When my girls were tweens, I taped a copy of these Scriptures to the wall in each of their rooms. Take a verse a week, working your way down through the list and praying these vital truths over you and your family.

_____

_____

_____

4. Ask God to help you see the unique gifts He has placed in your children, and ask Him for the wisdom to help you nurture these gifts in your kids. This is another detail of

importance to add to that journal. Imagine what a wonderful gift you will have to give your kids on their first day at college or on their wedding day.

_____

_____

_____

5. One thing I've become diligent about doing is writing down those moments when God visibly moves in my life or my family. Like the stories about Leslie's movie request or Rachel's chair. Be sure to write these kinds of happenings down in your child's journal. They'll be precious stories to read to your kids as they get older and a beautiful legacy for your children to share with your grandchildren.

_____

_____

_____

Prayer

My precious friend, I want to do something a little different at the end of this chapter. One of my favorite prayers that I've prayed for my husband and my daughters for years is straight out of Ephesians 3:14-21. Below is a paraphrase for you to pray. After you read it, keep reading. You'll find another way to pray this powerful Scripture.

Glorious Father of heaven and earth, my Lord God, I kneel before You and ask You to strengthen me for this high calling of motherhood through Your Son, Jesus, who lives and dwells in my inner being. Help me to be rooted and established in Your powerful love, Lord—Your love that is so wide and long and high and deep that I can barely grasp it. Lord, fill me to overflowing with Your Holy Spirit and with Your presence. Lord God, You are all I need, and You are more than able to help me and to do even more than I ask. I trust You with my life and with the lives of my children. For You are glorious and mighty. In Your great name I pray, Lord Jesus. Amen!

Use the *New International Version* (*NIV*) translation below and insert the name of your child, your spouse or anyone who you are praying will know the love of Jesus that transforms us. To Him be all the glory and praise!

For this reason I kneel before the Father, from whom every family in heaven and on earth derives its name. I pray that out of his glorious riches he may strengthen you, _____, with power through his Spirit in your inner being, so that Christ may dwell in your hearts through faith. And I pray that you, _____, being rooted and established in love, may have power, together with all the Lord's holy people, to grasp how wide and long and high and deep is the love of Christ, and to know this love that surpasses knowledge—that you, _____, may be filled to the measure of all the fullness of God. Now to Him who is able to do immeasurably more than all we ask or imagine, according to His power that is at work within us, to Him be glory in the church and in Christ Jesus throughout all generations, for ever and ever! Amen.

Respecting Dad

You know what's amazing yet absolutely baffling but so very God? The stronger we stand in who we are in Jesus, the more attractive we become. That's because we become true lamps that shine in the darkness. We become people of Jesus who exemplify integrity and honor. Let this truth, the truth of Jesus, live in you. Let it shine on your children and on their dad, because it is your greatest testimony and more powerful than anything you can say. This is the heart of 1 Peter 3:1-2. I love how *THE MESSAGE* paraphrases this truth:

There are husbands who, indifferent as they are to any words about God, will be captivated by your life of holy beauty.

My friend, live a life that impacts others by being real in your faith, and it won't be just your husband that you draw to Christ.

EIGHT

Triumphant Kids

Praying for Our Kids: Their Friends, Their Safety and Their Future

Lynn

Do not be overcome by evil, but overcome evil with good.
ROMANS 12:21

It started with a pound of hamburger.

Yep, I discovered a door of trust and a bridge to relationships, as well as a ton of laughter, opened up in our home when I was in the kitchen with a pound of ground beef. In the very early years of parenting both my son and my daughter, I committed to making my home a place where my children's friends were always welcome. As my kids grew, and even now as my daughter is a senior in high school, kids unexpectedly show up at our house to hang out.

As the noise enters the house, I ask, "How was your day?" followed by, "Are you hungry?" The answer to the first question often varies, but the answer to the second is always a loud and exuberant yes!

Thus the hamburger, and 20 minutes later, we have tacos for everyone. I've become known in teen circles around my town as Mexican-Food Mama. The teens chide me as they walk in, asking, "Hey, are we having tacos?" knowing full well what the answer will be. I smile at their kidding around and thank our Lord that I am accepted into their highly stressful and culturally challenging world. I am a voice in their lives. And it all started with a taco. Who knew?

The Home with the Open Door

What I've slowly realized is that, almost by accident, I've created a soft place to land for my children and their friends. Over the years, while kids munched on tacos and tortilla chips, I lingered with them in the kitchen, participating in something rare and special. I became part of their world, learning about their friendships and their families. I joined in laughter as they relived some crazy antic that took place in the drama class, and I empathized with them as they conveyed their complaints about their school projects, their challenging teachers and their troubles at home. My daughter and her best friend included me as they talked about their fears and concerns for students who were choosing the troubled path of drugs, and they shared their concern and pain with me about a friend of theirs who had decided to have sex with her boyfriend.

Over time and with intention, I've built relationships with these kids. I've welcomed them to step through our open door, and I have loved each one of them. My token offering of a taco turned out to be a rich investment in a number of young people. I've developed relationships through love and acceptance by purposely leaving judgments about these kids' clothes, music choices, sexual identities, hairstyles, etc., at the front door. I'm a safe adult in a world in which many kids don't know what it feels like.

I knew my son's friends, and now I know my daughter's teenaged friends, by name. I know their stories, struggles, hopes and dreams. Because I've chosen to be the keeper of the open door, I've been offered an unlikely friendship. I'm often invited by my daughter's friends to attend plays with the crowd, to see a movie or to do something else. There are times when I'm the only adult included in these young people's adventures, which sometimes feels weird. But this blonde, five-foot-four, older mom joins the throng of kids and participates in their culture.

Being the parent with the open door actually reduces my mom-stress. I know where my child is, and I know whom she is with. The open door also allows me something far more important: it lets me know what to pray for my daughter and her friends as they try to navigate the difficulties of adolescence.

I think it goes without saying that friendships bear significant influence on our children's choices, on how they process life and on how they react to the world around them. As a praying mom, I'm compelled to bring these teens before God in prayer, and more importantly, I bring my son and daughter before God with requests, concerns and hopes. I want God's wisdom, power and love to influence and impact my children and their friends. So I pray words from a mother's heart.

Having been a mom now for more than 30 years, I'm convinced that a mother's prayer is one of the most powerful on earth. Read this passage from James with me: "The prayer of a righteous man [woman] is powerful and effective" (5:16). My friends, this passage is amplified when a mom whispers words filled with passion, seeking God's protection, intervention and wisdom for her children.

A Prayer Warrior, Not a Worrier

There is a battle for our children. The battle is real but often so subtle that it's difficult to recognize. However, we as believers know the God of the universe. We live in relationship with Him and walk in God-sized confidence, and the Lord expects us to intercede for our children. He waits to answer our earnest pleadings powerfully and effectively. How do I know this? I've experienced God's faithful answers to my simple yet heartfelt prayers for my kids over and again.

Let me share a recent instance.

Several months ago my daughter came home from school absolutely distraught, tears flowing and almost inconsolable. A certain teenage boy at school had decided to make my daughter the target of his verbal barbs. From my daughter's perspective this boy's sole purpose in life was to make her miserable. His caustic words hit their mark, challenging her confidence, bruising her self-worth. If I could have X-rayed my daughter's heart at that time, I would have discovered that it was torn and bleeding.

This went on for days, then weeks and for several months. Well, I'll tell you what—when our child endures something such as bullying, the mama bear in us moms rises up and roars with ferocity. My friends, the circumstances were such for us that a direct confrontation with this kid was not possible. But that mattered little to me, because I'm friends with a great big God. I began to pray.

I will share with you that I prayed with passion and emotion, and I prayed for weeks. It was laborious praying, filled with a relentless conviction to surround my daughter with God's power and to change her circumstances. I prayed every morning for her as I stood on the driveway in front of our home, watching her drive toward school. I'm quite certain the neighbors must have been perplexed as they watched me speak aloud toward the car, my hand raised as the vehicle proceeded up the street.

I prayed something like this:

Lord, my holy God,

This very moment I'm asking for Your presence to surround Caitie. Lord, go with her into the halls of her high school. Father, in the name of Jesus I take authority from the enemy who is speaking lies into my daughter's heart and mind. I renounce any lies that my daughter believes, such as she is insignificant. I bind the enemy who has told her that she is ugly, stupid or a fool. O Holy Spirit, rush with this car and remove thoughts of insecurity or fear from my daughter. Lord, I bind this boy at her school who, out of his own fear and insecurity, pours words of harm into my daughter. Lord, I surround him, and through Your power I pray that he is unable to speak any evil into my daughter or to other students about my daughter. Move in his life to reveal to him Your love for him this day.

Powerful Lord, my Father, Abba, now I hold up my daughter, Caitie, and in place of the lies, I ask You to affirm her.

Place Your truth in her. Let others, including this boy, only say things about her and to her that are truthful and uplifting. When this young man hears her name, change his thoughts toward her to be good and not evil. When her name is spoken, prompt him to affirm her and to build up her character. Lord, speak through her friends to break the lies and to pour Your truth into my girl. Father, speak gently into my girl, and remind her that she is beautiful. She is a daughter of the King. She is confident in her identity. She is a believer in truth and justice. Affirm her worth, and let her see herself as You view her.

Affirm, protect, love on her with passion, and reveal Yourself to her daily. I pray this in the name of Jesus and by His authority and power. Amen.

I continued to pray similarly in my quiet time with God later in the morning. I prayed for my daughter in this manner throughout each day for weeks. It was arduous praying, and at times I felt worn out, but my passion for change, through the hand of the Lord, fueled my words and commitment.

Recently, late in the evening my daughter returned from a restaurant where she had met several of her friends for dinner. She walked into my room where I was reading. "Mom," she said, "you are not going to believe what happened tonight."

I looked up from my book, "What?"

She mentioned the names of the young people who had been at dinner. I winced when she mentioned the last name—that of her nemesis. She then said, "Mom, when it was time to leave the restaurant, this kid said to the group, 'I want Caitie to drive me home.' I reluctantly agreed, because there wasn't really another alternative. We got into the car, and I was ready to do battle with this kid because I thought he was going to start right in with his trash talk. I tensed up, gripping the steering wheel, and pulled out of the parking lot.

"Mom, he looked at me and then he proceeded to apologize for treating me so badly and for being mean. Then he said he wanted to be friends. Can you believe it?"

I looked at my child. A smile filled my face, and I said, "Oh, honey, I'm so glad." I followed right up with, "I have to tell you that I'm not surprised, because I've been praying for this very thing."

Relief and hope displayed across my daughter's face. It felt as though the battle was finally over. She smiled at me with peace in her eyes, leaned over, kissed my forehead, turned and left the room.

All was right with the world.

My heart filled, and tears sprang to my eyes. I began praying, "Oh, Abba Daddy, thank You for Your kind favor. Thank You for Your fathomless love and for Your care for my child." I prayed for days after that, giving praise and thanks that the God of the universe loves me and my daughter.

Of course, not all our prayers are answered in dramatic fashion or even in the manner we are seeking, but it is our calling as mothers to pray, because if we are not praying for our kids by name, then who is? It is our high privilege to pray for our children and to bring their lives before God, fully trusting the Lord that He has every minute of every day of our kids' lives in the palm of His hand.

My fellow mom, let's choose this day to pray as warriors and to leave our worry behind us. Let's choose to love our children's friends and to pray for their relationships. Let's pray with passion and power and then watch all that God will do, just because we asked. We might be the humble mothers who change the destiny of a nation through praying for the young lives that God has brought into our sphere of influence.

Setting the Stage

I press on toward the goal to win the prize for which God has called me heavenward in Christ Jesus.

PHILIPPIANS 3:14

When my son, Brad, was young, he loved Hot Wheels toy cars. We must have owned a bazillion of these tiny four-wheeled critters. These miniature vehicles would randomly appear in cupboards, be stuffed into pants pockets, be buried in the garden, sink down into the bathwater at bath time, and show up in the washing machine after they came out of said pants' pockets. I've stepped on, sat on and kicked at least a thousand of these potentially dangerous little beasts as they were strewn across the house. Stepping on one at a brisk pace is a potential invitation to a chiropractic appointment. I know that I grumbled a few words under my breath as I flung a few of the tiny four-wheeled trinkets back into the toy box. But as I remember these cars today, I smile. I think of the little motor sounds my son made as he drove them across the kitchen floor. And as I reminisce back to that time, I see in my mind's eye my boy's tiny back hunched over a car that he was pushing with his chubby hand toward some impending crash. It's this memory of my little guy playing cars that reminds me just how young he was when I began to pray something very specific for him and to pray for someone I would not meet for years—his wife.

It may seem strange that I was praying for my then-seven-year-old's wife, but think with me for a moment. Our children's spouses, their marriage and in-laws will form the most significant relationships, next to the one they have with Jesus, that our kids will navigate throughout their lives. As a young mom, I wasn't leaving people this important to chance. I began to pray for my son's wife in detail, asking the Lord to bring him the woman of his dreams and praying that this woman would be a believer. I asked God to reveal her to him and to cover their relationship with His favor. I prayed regularly for this particular woman whom I would not meet for years.

Right behind my prayers for this unknown girl, I prayed for her family. In-laws can make or break a couple. And in a selfish way, I wanted to really like my son's in-laws. I prayed that they would be great people to hang around with, that our families would blend and that we would enjoy one another. I prayed that they would edify my son and my daughter-in-law's marriage. Over the years I prayed about a great number of details regarding my son's future. And I've been praying in the same way for my daughter since she was a baby.

When you speak to God about people like your in-laws for a long time, it's really a neat moment when you finally meet them. For me that was last year when my son married. Brad's new wife is delightful. She makes my son a better man, and I love her deeply. I also love her family, and I especially love that they are really fun.

I will always pray for my son and his new wife as they walk through this newly begun marriage journey. They have a young faith in God that will require maturing, as well as all the typical adjustments of the newly married, and more recently a little one is now on the way. But I have watched God's faithfulness, and I know that He is walking with them, because I asked Him to.

Mom, perhaps right now you are walking the early and middle years of child rearing, when parenting is lonely. You are physically and emotionally exhausted, and you feel as though everything you are trying to do in your child is not working. Take heart, and remember the faithfulness of our God toward our children.

Every moment that we pour into our little people, every time we capture a teachable moment, every word of prayer we lift up, every day we model our faith in the mundane ordinary as well as the extravagant extraordinary, it is worth it. The payoff comes years and years later as our kids become young adults. They will walk from our homes into their adult lives, fully equipped men and women who will pass the legacy of faith to the next generation.

For the LORD is good. His unfailing love continues forever, and his faithfulness continues to each generation (Ps. 100:5, *NLT*).

Discovery

Mom, set aside your unfolded laundry for a moment. Grab a hot or cold tea and your Bible, and join me as we discover a few aspects of God's faithfulness. "Mothers hold their children's hands for a short while but their hearts forever" (author unknown).

1. Describe an environment that you would consider a "safe place to land" for your children.

   _____

   _____

   _____

   _____

2. Can you remember someone's home from your childhood that was an "open-door home" in which kids were welcome? Consider what unique aspects and people contributed to that feeling you had of being welcome. What are those aspects? Can you bring them into your home?

   _____

   _____

   _____

   _____

3. Write down each of your children's names. Under their names write down their best friend's name, then follow that with the names of the kids who spend a significant amount of time with your children and/or those who bear influence upon them. Use this as a prayer prompt in your quiet time with the Lord.

   _____

   _____

   _____

4. This week ask your children about their friends. Ask your children how you could pray for their friendships. Pray for their concerns this week. Give God thanks for answers to prayer, and share those answers with your son or daughter.

_____

_____

_____

5. Consider what attributes you are hoping for in your children's future spouses, their in-laws and their marriage relationships. Write these down and then date your paper and save it. In the future, such as on your child's wedding day, you can look back upon this list and experience God's faithfulness.

_____

_____

_____

6. Look up Matthew 19:14-15. What does this passage say to you?

_____

_____

_____

Prayer

O Lord, my holy God, today I bring our home before You. Father, may our house be a place in which our children feel they are loved, treasured and safe to live authentically. Let our home be a place in which it's okay to be messy and a place in which friends are welcome. Lord, never let me see my children as an inconvenience. Every day let me be conscious that You have only lent them to me for a short time, and that I need to use that time wisely. Teach me how to use my influence, my love and all my abilities to mold my children into young men and women of character, grace and love. Mostly, Lord, let me impart to them a contagious love for Your Son, Jesus.

Father, let our house be a place of laughter, filled with forgiveness, compassion and unending adventure. Always allow me to be there with a taco, a smile, a hug and words of wisdom and grace. Lord, let Your Holy Spirit flow through me and out to my children and their friends. Let them catch a glimpse of You in our home and in our hearts. Lord, create in my kids a love for Jesus that impacts our home, their friends and one day their spouses, their in-laws and the world. Protect my kids, provide for them and prepare their lives for all You have for them. I thank You for this crazy, unexpected, astonishing and heart-filled gift of motherhood. Help me to be the best mother I can be. In Jesus' powerful and holy name. Amen.

Respecting Dad

I know that for many men it can be increasingly challenging to remain engaged in their children's lives as the kids become older. A father's work commitments can get in the way. Scheduling of our children's extracurricular activities also change. Be diligent to encourage Dad to discover new activities and moments in which he can spend time with the kids, developing trust and authentic relationship. Encourage him to spend time with his children's friends as well.

As a mom, take the initiative and open the door of your home. Make the kids welcome, and include Dad as much as he wants to participate. This kind of gentle respect goes a long way in Dad's eyes.

NINE

Challenging Kids

Handling Tough Questions, Confusing Situations and Special Needs

Dineen

*Those who are victorious will inherit all this,
and I will be their God and they will be my children.*
REVELATION 21:7

Dear one, this is most likely the hardest yet easiest chapter for me to write in this book. Difficult because of its subject matter but easy since, having walked through depression and cancer with my youngest daughter, my heart is with any mom who faces seemingly impossible challenges. Even if you're not in a tough place with your kids right now, walk with me and let me explain a journey that for me still continues.

Before Lynn and I began planning this book, I knew that one chapter would need to be about the tough questions our children ask us, about the confusion of living in a spiritually mismatched home and how all this gets even tougher when our children have emotional, physical or mental needs.

I've shared tidbits with you about my daughter's successful battle with cancer, but I'll tell you now, the emotional aftermath of her recovery and her depression were the most difficult parts of this challenge. Some days I wondered how things would ever get better. I pictured a future looming with an unchanging and unrelenting pattern of mere survival and not much hope.

But during this time my daughter and I learned some of our greatest lessons of faith. We learned that a season of difficulty and trial didn't define our entire lives. We learned that hope placed in Jesus rather than in our ever-changing circumstances would never fail. We learned that the value and impact of a precious moment could carry us through a day and shore up those places where hope lagged.

We learned that our God is bigger than any issue we may face and has an answer for every question. Even the toughest ones.

The Big *Why*?

I can do all things through him who strengthens me.
PHILIPPIANS 4:13 (*ESV*)

As a teenager I babysat a little boy whose favorite word was "why." Every answer I gave him seemed to lead his curious little brain to another question. Thankfully, most of his questions were easy to handle, even if I had to just tell him, "I don't know why."

Most of the questions we get from our kids are pretty manageable, but sometimes, their questions will push us beyond our own ability and right into the presence of the Holy Spirit. Thankfully, God's wisdom and guidance are readily available for us at the throne of grace (see Heb. 4:16). We don't have to have all the answers, because God does.

Of all the questions, one of the biggies is, "Why doesn't Daddy love Jesus?" Lynn shared in chapter 3 how she answered this question when her daughter, Caitie, asked it. I've dealt with the same question from both my daughters in much the same way Lynn did, with the goal to keep their love and respect for Dad intact but also to enlist them in the mission to pray for their dad to know Jesus.

Above all, we want to help our children understand why we should and how we can love without judgment and to let our prayers and hope spring from this place. Look at this precious story I received from a woman named Kendra:

> My son and I watched *Polar Express* together. When the movie ended, we talked about how he doesn't believe in Santa. I never outright confessed to his suspicion that parents *are* Santa, but instead I talked with him about how he shouldn't ruin it for other kids who still believe. Christmas is a joyous and fun time, and if you tell kids there is no Santa, you will be taking some of the joy away from them, and that's just mean.
>
> When I asked him about the true spirit of Christmas, he replied, "I don't believe in Santa, but I believe in Jesus!" What an awesome moment for me! He talked about how Easter was important too, and he asked me questions about the resurrection and where Jesus is now. He said we should go to where the tomb is so that maybe we could see Him!
>
> But all of this led him to talk about how Dad does not believe in Jesus. Then he started to cry when he told me that Dad isn't going to heaven. We sobbed together for a few minutes. I could see the worry on his face. I comforted him by telling him that his job is to pray for Dad, that God loves his dad even more than either of us do and that He wants Dad to believe in Jesus even more than we do. So we are going to pray and let God work on Dad's heart.
>
> Oh, such a bittersweet moment for me. Nostalgic that my little boy no longer believes in Santa Claus, happy and relieved that the same little boy is starting to understand what it means to know Jesus, but oh so sad that an eight-year-old boy has to wrestle with the complex concept of his daddy's salvation. Lastly, so very grateful that God has been working on my little boy's heart without a lot of help from me and despite a dad that cannot allow himself to believe in the same things we do. It's these small slices of time that I pray and prepare for.

One of the most difficult questions my daughter Leslie asked me was in regard to her cancer. Before her diagnosis, we'd spent a great year together doing homeschooling and helping her overcome her depression. She felt good, was on the right track and for the first time in her life was excited about starting school—high school. When the school year started, she made friends fast and finally seemed to be coming into her own. We all thought the worst was behind us.

Then the headaches set in, and we were soon on the fast track to a diagnosis of a malignant brain tumor, then to surgeries and treatment. Leslie's bright start fizzled into spinning chaos.

One day in the car, on one of our many trips between home and the doctor's office, the toughest question she ever asked me came:

"Why did God let this happen to me?"

I'd made peace with this question myself, but I'd had multiple years to walk with God and to come to understand His character and the truth of Roman 8:28. How could I pour all that had taken me years to learn into one simple answer to help my little girl?

I prayed. I prayed hard. Above all I wanted my words to reassure her that she would be okay. I wanted her to understand the truth of 2 Corinthians 4:16-18:

Therefore we do not lose heart. Though outwardly we are wasting away, yet inwardly we are being renewed day by day. For our light and momentary troubles are achieving for us an eternal glory that far outweighs them all. So we fix our eyes not on what is seen, but on what is unseen, since what is seen is temporary, but what is unseen is eternal.

The first thing I shared with her was the truth of Romans 8:28, that God works in all things for our good and to bring good from them. I told her that just as she had overcome her depression, with God's help she would overcome this too. In many ways her battle with depression had strengthened and prepared her for the battle that now lay before her. She clung to

Philippians 4:13 as her life verse. Today I look at my daughter and see that this Scripture is the truth of her life—that all she has overcome she has done through Christ who continues to strengthen her.

How we look at the trials, challenges and discomforts of life will directly affect the way we walk through them, and how we walk through them will directly educate our children. Our trials, challenges and discomforts are purposed or repurposed by God for our good.

And the fruit of one trial becomes the strength of the next.

Give Yourself and Your Child a Break

Sometimes our greatest challenge as moms is realizing we can't fix things—and we can't "fix" our children. For me this battle waged during the worst times of my daughter's depression. I would pray and beg God to change her, fix her, heal her—anything I could think of. Yet the battle raged on.

My prayers began to change to, "Lord, help me be the mother Leslie needs right now. Give me the strength to walk through this day with her." My dear friend, there were times when I honestly didn't know how to go on and could only pray, "Lord, I have nothing left. Today it has to be all You."

God never failed to show up and to give me the strength I desperately needed to love my daughter through her ordeal. He taught me that a hope placed in Jesus never fails and that as overwhelming as our situation was at the time, it wasn't the complete picture—just a small slice of the big picture that would soon change. Over time we started to have more good days than bad, and my hope for my daughter to have a normal life and a future burst within me like the seed of a flower soaked in the first spring rains.

I know that in the deepest places of pain we forget there is life beyond the dark place we are in. There is always a place of light and hope with God, even in the middle of our darkest storms. My precious friend, for your sake and for your child's, don't let this affliction, this trial, this challenge be the definition of you and your child. Take a break; breathe and laugh. As much as you need a break, your child probably does too. Do something fun.

To this day one of my daughters' fondest memories was of a sock fight. We were living in Europe, the girls were struggling to adjust to the culture, and language and life had become just plain hard. I walked into my bedroom with a basketful of folded laundry and heard my girls playing above in the loft.

Those pairs of balled-up socks just beckoned to be tossed. So I tossed them. Soon every pair of socks that my husband owned became fuzzy missiles thrown back and forth as in a snowball fight. We all needed a break from our struggle. We needed to laugh and remember what laughter felt like. We needed to love each other.

There is no stronger force on this earth than God's love. That love arrived in a small swaddled bundle over 2,000 years ago, took 33 years to season and prepare and then exploded beyond human understanding in a moment in time that none of us will ever forget.

He is our truth, He is our life, He is our hope. God's love. Our Jesus.

Treasure the Moments

Therefore we do not lose heart. Though outwardly we are wasting away, yet inwardly we are being renewed day by day. For our light and momentary troubles are achieving for us an eternal glory that far outweighs them all. So we fix our eyes not on what is seen, but on what is unseen, since what is seen is temporary, but what is unseen is eternal.

2 CORINTHIANS 4:16-18

One of the greatest lessons I learned through my daughter's depression and cancer ordeals was the importance of moments— moments that came suddenly and unexpectedly into our ongoing situation and stood out significantly because they were full of God's love and hope.

When we face ongoing challenges and trials, we run the danger of seeing only what is in front of us—our world becomes defined by our situation. The danger in this is that we risk missing those moments when God shows up (even in a sock fight!). We miss that moment of laughter when we didn't think laughter was possible. Or the hug from a spouse you didn't think loved you anymore. Or the first glimmer of repentance in a wayward teen who is desperate to be loved.

The way we walk through the trials and challenges of life, whether they are our own or our children's, directly affects our kids. If our children can see that our hope is planted firmly in Jesus during these times, they will learn to follow our example. Dare I say that this may be one of the most crucial lessons we ever pass on to our children, since this is a life skill they will need as adults?

Will you help your children to be the house built on the solid foundation that will remain standing through the storm (see Luke 6:48)? Or will they be the waves blown to and fro by the winds of doubt?

Listen in on this precious mom's story of victory and restoration as she walked with her daughter through the aftermath of an abusive and traumatic marriage:

> I have been seeing this family counselor for a few weeks now. I am not sure if she is a Christian or not—she was "appointed" to me by the police for free. My daughter and I got 10 sessions each. Anyway, I saw her several times, and then about two weeks ago she saw my daughter for the first time. The counselor spent an hour talking with my daughter about our situation as my daughter drew things for her. So I was very anxious today to find out what the counselor had found out about how my daughter was doing in light of our divorce.
>
> The counselor said, "Elizabeth has a very solid foundation."
>
> I was thinking, *Wow, I bet she does. Her foundation is in Christ.*
>
> Then the counselor said, "Elizabeth has a very steady energy about herself."
>
> That's the Holy Spirit working in her.

"Elizabeth has been exposed to trauma, but she has not been traumatized by it."

She has been in the fire, but she has not been burned (remember Daniel).

"She is like a little boat in the middle of the storm that has been able to float through the storm, yes, through the waves and the wind, but because she has this solid center, she has been able to stay afloat until the storm has calmed down."

Amen; I have heard this story somewhere else.

Then the counselor said, "Continue taking her to church."

Oh, yes, I will!

"Let her pray for her dad, because it is a very positive flow of energy for her."

Oh, yes, it is indeed!

The counselor also said that I am doing exceptionally well and don't need any more counseling, and neither does my daughter. Thank God!

I thought it was great to hear her feedback in all these psychological and worldly terms that she was using that yet so powerfully reflected the work of God and the Holy Spirit in our lives. It was like God showed up and opened my eyes to yet even more things that He has done for me without my even realizing it.

Joni Erickson Tada once said, "Faith isn't the ability to believe long and far into the misty future. It's simply taking God at His Word and taking the next step." Just take the next step, my dear friend, and trust God for the rest. I promise, He won't disappoint you.

Discovery

My dear fellow mom, thank you for walking through this chapter with me. I think this was the most emotional one, because it tapped some tender areas in my heart. I pray with the depths of my love for you that it brings you comfort and hope.

We need that in our rough times, don't we? Especially when our child's struggle is ongoing. Take heart, my friend. God is with you all the way. He knows your needs and will take care of you.

1. Take your time looking up these Scriptures, and let them settle into your heart. Use more than one translation if it will help you get an even deeper understanding of what and who our hope is. Jot down next to each verse what you want most to remember.

   Jeremiah 29:11:

   _____

   _____

   Isaiah 40:31:

   _____

   _____

   Psalm 25:4-5:

   _____

   _____

   Romans 5:5:

   _____

   _____

   Romans 8:24-25:

   _____

   _____

2. What have been the most challenging questions that your
    children have asked you? Are you grappling to answer such
    a question right now? Ask the Holy Spirit for wisdom, for
    guidance from key Scriptures and for a friend or mentor at
    church who can help you.

    _____

    _____

    _____

3. Are you trying to handle everything on your own? Write
    down everything that you're dealing with. How about
    joining a women's group for Bible study and prayer
    support to keep you from getting isolated? I know that's
    hard to do, especially when you feel that you're barely
    keeping your head above water, but trust me, it's the best
    thing for you. Let some ladies love on you and support you
    with prayer.

    _____

    _____

    _____

4. Think of several ways that you and your kids can have some
    fun, even if it's in your own back yard. Make a list. Enter
    your child's world with the goal to play and laugh together.
    No agenda, no lectures, no worrying. Ask God to bless this
    time and to give you more opportunities to do this.

    _____

    _____

    _____

5. Are you in tune with those precious moments that make all the difference in our lives? Ask the Holy Spirit to help you be more aware so that you don't miss out on them. More moments to add to your journal!

_____

_____

_____

Prayer

Abba, You know the condition of my heart better than anyone does. Some days I wonder how I'm going to take one more step. Show me, Lord, how to depend on Your strength and not on my own. Lord Jesus, forgive me for doubting You and for doubting Your presence with me. Holy Spirit, flood me with new strength, new belief, new ways to pray for my children and their special needs, and when the doubting darkness threatens again, remind me that You are right there, renewing my strength and my mind. Restore to me the joy of Your salvation.

Holy Spirit, I give You complete reign over my thoughts, because Romans 8:6 says that a mind controlled by the Spirit is life and peace. I want life, Lord! I want peace! Help me to walk through each day with complete and total trust in You. In Your holy name, Jesus. Amen!

Respecting Dad

My dear reader, I have one more story for you. One day when my family was in the early stages of our daughter's cancer ordeal, my husband and I stood in the kitchen, our hearts heavy with what lay before our daughter. I shared with my husband that God had told me she would be okay. I wanted to offer my husband the same comfort and reassurance that God had given me. I wish I could tell you that it meant something to him. He simply smiled and said, "That's fine for you." I gave him a hug and prayed that the physical contact would give him comfort instead.

How we walk through a trial will look very different from how your children's father will walk through this challenge. You and I have a mighty God to lean on. Their dad, most likely, only has you. I know that your hands are already full with whatever situation you are dealing with, but try to find ways to keep unity between you and their father. Adversity has a nasty way of pulling people apart. Stay alert and find ways to include Dad in whatever process or treatment or life adjustment your child is going through. You are a team, and your child needs your solidarity now more than ever. When life is no longer normal, moments of normalcy can be a great gift and comfort.

TEN

Legacy Kids

Jesus for the Generations

Lynn

Know therefore that the LORD your God is God; he is the faithful God, keeping his covenant of love to a thousand generations of those who love him and keep his commands.

DEUTERONOMY 7:9

When I speak at events, I often bring my Daily Bible with me. I share with the audience how this single book has changed my entire life. I've read through this Bible every year for more than 14 years. You may yawn and think how boring it would be to read the same thing over and over, and you might be right. However, it never ceases to amaze me how God consistently reveals new understanding through His Word. I can't wait to open it up every morning and allow God to lead me to something new.

I want to share with you a recent encounter I had with a Scripture passage. It's a passage with which I am familiar, but God spoke its value and meaning into my life in a brand-new way. Would you please join me in the garden?

As I write this final chapter, it's a beautiful summer morning. Earlier this morning, I went outside to sit in my backyard garden and to read my Daily Bible. The New Testament passage for today's portion was in Acts 16. Let's read it together:

> Paul went first to Derbe and then to Lystra, where there was a young disciple named Timothy. His mother was a Jewish believer, but his father was a Greek (Acts 16:1, *NLT*).

I read this single sentence and felt as if God were gripping my spirit. He held my full attention, because for the first time I realized that Timothy's parents were spiritually mismatched. His mother was a Jewish believer, and his father a Gentile, an unbeliever. Could it be that there were parents just like you and me mentioned in the Bible?

I read the verse again and thought about how the people of Greece in biblical time were considered studied and cerebral. Yep, that would describe my husband. And Timothy's mother, she was a believer. The narrative of Timothy's mom and dad was nearly a description of my marriage. I read the verse again, and it was as if God spoke to my heart, "See, Lynn, being spiritually mismatched is nothing new."

Whoa. Why hadn't I fully comprehended this passage of Scripture before now? By this point, I was completely intrigued, and I continued to read. The passage describes this young man, Timothy:

> Timothy was well thought of by the believers in Lystra and Iconium (Acts 16:2, *NLT*).

Wow, I thought to myself, *Timothy must have been raised right.* And then it hit me. I had a vague recollection of a passage of Scripture somewhere in the Bible that described Timothy's mother. So I looked it up. It's in 2 Timothy, where Paul writes a letter to Timothy. Listen in:

> I remember your genuine faith, for you share the faith that first filled your grandmother Lois and your mother, Eunice. And I know that same faith continues strong in you (2 Tim. 1:5, *NLT*).

My heart soared as the meaning of these words landed on my soul. Timothy had been raised in a spiritually mismatched home. His genuine faith was born out of his mother's and his grandmother's faith. Neat.

I used to think that being spiritually mismatched was a rare condition for married believers. For years I was of the opinion that the Bible only focused on married couples as two believers. In fact, for years I think I've been hung up on 2 Corinthians 6:14, "Do not be unequally yoked . . ." (*ESV*).

The enemy had me completely duped, convinced that my marriage to my unbelieving spouse was a sin of insurmountable consequence and because of my disobedience, I must bear this cross until the day I die. I allowed that single verse to overshadow every other passage that is written for people living in relationships just like yours and mine. And as a side note, I completely understand God's reason for 2 Corinthians 6:14, because a spiritually mismatched marriage is a very difficult road to travel. Yet now, after more than 20 years walking in my unique marriage and walking with God, I can say with utter confidence, "God knows what He is doing, even in a spiritual mismatch."

From the days of antiquity until the end of the age, there have been and will always be marriages between believers and unbelievers. Regardless of how we arrived in our unequally yoked marriage, we are part of God's plans and our spiritually mismatched homes are vital to His purposes. These matches are not our misfortune. Our wise King works through us, the believers, in these unique relationships with absolute intention. There are eternities at stake, and God is relentless in His desire to reveal Himself to the unsaved.

Now think about Timothy's mother, Eunice. Her personal name when translated from the Greek actually means "victorious."

Did you get that, my friends? Victorious! Oh, how like God to encourage us further by shouting that this believing mom is victorious.

I think this passage especially speaks to us mothers who are raising boys. As our boys grow older, they tend to be more and more like their father. Their dad's ideas, opinions and beliefs gain prominence in our boys' minds as they grow into young men. But take courage, faithful mom, because God placed this passage in His holy Word to show you that the intentional love and teaching that you pour into your young men and women make every bit of difference.

We are victorious through the power of Jesus Christ.

Pondering this passage, I marveled that God had chosen to speak to me and to all of us who are walking this path of unique motherhood. He recognizes how utterly important our calling is to our kids and even to our grandkids. God knows that it's the believing moms who instruct and love the next generation into the saving truth of Jesus Christ. Doing this is scary at times, yet it's the greatest honor of our entire life and the most fantastic adventure we will ever live.

I can tell you that I have read this passage of Scripture over and over in the many years of my study of God's Word. But it wasn't until now that the Holy Spirit truly brought about its full meaning and its implication for my life. Tears sprang to my eyes as I pondered the depths of God's love for me and for each of my children. His faithfulness is unrelenting, year after year.

I dabbed at my eyes, but God wasn't finished. So, to outshine Himself, as if that is possible, God revealed more as I read further about Eunice.

At the end of the third chapter of 2 Timothy, Paul mentions Eunice and Lois, Timothy's grandmother, once again. In this particular letter to Timothy, Paul gives the young man wise counsel as well as his life's mission:

> But you must remain faithful to the things you have been taught. You know they are true, for you know you can trust those who taught you. You have been taught the holy Scriptures from childhood, and they have given you the wisdom to receive the salvation that comes by trusting in Christ Jesus (2 Tim. 3:14-15, *NLT*).

These words are for us. This is Paul's assurance that our years of relentlessly pouring Jesus into our kids will result in passing the wisdom to receive the salvation that comes by trusting in Christ Jesus.

Every prayer that we uttered, every slim and fleeting teachable moment that we seized, every opportunity in which we spoke God's Word into our kids and modeled our faith *will not be wasted*. Like most things in God's economy, these investments take time. Our efforts pay off long after our children leave our home. And we may never see the final outcome of our tears, our labors, our hard work this side of heaven. But I promise you, our efforts are not fruitless nor in vain.

As we near the end of our parenting journey, I'm impressed strongly by the Spirit to speak into your life what Paul spoke into Timothy: Fight the good fight of the faith. Take hold of the eternal life to which you were called. Remember your genuine faith, for you share the faith with all those who have gone before you. And I know that same faith continues strongly in you. This is why I remind you to fan into flame the spiritual gifts God gave you. For God has not given us a spirit of fear and timidity but of power, love and self-discipline.

My dearest mom, the last sentence of Paul's charge to Timothy has been my lifeline for years. Memorize this passage (2 Tim. 1:7, *NLT*). Let it become real to you, and live boldly, without fear. Be filled with God's power and His unfathomable, unfailing love. Then you will discover that living a life of selflessness for your family is your ultimate joy. This kind of life is thriving in love.

One Life

Her children stand and bless her. Her husband praises her: "There are many virtuous and capable women in the world, but you surpass them all!" Charm is deceptive, and beauty does not last; but a woman who fears the LORD will be greatly praised. Reward her for all she has done. Let her deeds publicly declare her praise.

PROVERBS 31:28-31 (*NLT*)

As our book draws to a finish, I find myself feeling melancholy and a little sad to say goodbye. While contemplating the end of our time together, I've felt a bit unsettled, but why?

One morning several days ago, while wrestling with this troubled place in my heart—this book's ending—I went on one of my walk-'n'-prays. On this particular day, I took my unsettled feelings to the Lord.

"Lord," I prayed, "why do I feel as if we haven't finished the story yet? Father, what is it that You still want to say to every mother reading this book?"

Well, I'll tell you what. God showed up! He'd been waiting for me to ask this question, because once I did, immediately a string of words were impressed on my mind.

Those words were a letter.

As the words began to tumble into my soul, I sobbed. I sobbed and walked. I walked and sobbed. And when I typed the words you will read below, more tears slipped from my eyes.

God has asked me to share this letter with you, my dear fellow mom. It is deeply personal, from Him to you. God also gave me the structure, showing me to leave a line where you are to write your name. Find a pen and a quiet place to receive "The Letter to My Chosen Mother."

My Beloved _____,

I have loved you and your children since before you were born. I have treasured you and have been walking with you long before you knew I was there.

I stayed with you in the delivery room when you pushed through your labor. I stood near your head and marveled at the plans for this tiny life you were birthing, knowing that you were chosen to be this child's mother.

When you tickled your baby's feet and when giggles filled your heart, your laughter was worship in My ears.

I stood present in your child's bedroom when your brow was furrowed with deep lines of worry. You wiped the child to cool the fever as I held your child's hand and watched you work and whisper desperate prayers.

I heard every word.

When your little one waved to you on the first day of school, your tears I saw. You didn't know it, but at My command a legion of angels walked with that small one through the door of the school.

I saw the cruelty of teasing and bullying by other kids on the playground. And when your small one cried himself to sleep, I was the One who gently kissed the tears from his cheek and whispered words of joy and hope for his future into his dreams that night.

It was I who cheered with you, my beloved, at your child's first step, at her discovery of puppies and mud pies. It was I who watched over her while she slept and who thrilled with a proud chuckle at her first crush.

My love soared at your child's baptism, and My righteous anger flared when the enemy spoke lies of deception and destruction into our beautiful child.

When you failed or you didn't get a parenting moment quite right or even when sin caused pain or harm to those in your care, please know that every one of those moments I have redeemed. From those failures I will shine bright. I will use your child's pain to draw him to Me in his adult years.

I know you have felt overwhelmed, uncertain and ill-equipped for this mission of mothering, but I assure you that I stand at your side to love and protect you and those you treasure most. I love your children with a depth and ferocity you cannot conceive of this side of heaven.

Never doubt for one second that I am beside you. I am whispering words of wisdom into your ears, and when you feel all alone in training up your child, stop and allow yourself to feel My embrace. I am all around you, and I will never leave you nor forsake you.

Every effort, action, correction, instruction and emotion you pour into your children will prove itself out in the future. That is My promise. Cling to that in the difficult days. It is all worth it.

Beloved mother, you are the chosen one.

Your mission field is a divine calling, to which none other can compare. Your mothering is far more important to Me than feeding the hungry or serving in church or supporting missions to other countries. Your mission field is your home; it *is your husband and your children. This mission is for life, and this mission is eternal.*

Your mission is love.

This is your high and holy calling.

And this is My Word: your children will rise and call you blessed. Your husband, your children's father, will praise you, and, chosen mother of My heart, your strength, love and worship of Me will rise up, and you will surpass them all.

Your name and those of your children are written upon My heart.

—The Lord God Almighty

When you have a difficult day, when you feel as if you have failed your children or your husband or even failed in your faith, take out this letter, my friend. Allow God to love on you all over again.

A Calling

Mom, we won't have a perfect life—far from it. But it is a life filled with laughter and joy. Of course, there will be tears and at times, difficult struggles. But we are living for a higher purpose than we can comprehend. We will reach our golden years with gray hair and wrinkles but also with a twinkle in our eye, because we will have walked with God. We will have watched our children grow up and become parents themselves.

We will know Jesus as we reach our end of days, and regardless of our spouse's salvation choice, we will have lived lives destined to bring great honor and glory to God and to His Son, Jesus. We will have lived the everyday adventure with joy. We will have lived the abundant life.

We are the ordinary moms who did the extraordinary.

We gave Jesus to the generations.

Discovery

1. Read Acts 16:1-2. In verse 1 of this passage we discovered a spiritually mismatched relationship. In the second verse Timothy is described. How is he perceived by the people

of the nearby towns? How does this passage reflect on Timothy's mother and grandmother?

_____

_____

_____

2. Has 2 Corinthians 6:14 been a stumbling block in your faith walk? Please describe how.

_____

_____

_____

3. Look up Romans 8:1. Write it down. Then pray and ask God to place this passage in perspective and to allow you to live without condemnation and to walk in freedom.

_____

_____

_____

4. Take time to do a search and/or to research passages of Scripture that speak to those who live in spiritually mismatched marriages. List them.

_____

_____

_____

5. I shared with you how the passage in 2 Timothy 1:7 was a
    lifeline for me. What passage or passages have proven to be
    your lifeline?

    _____

    _____

    _____

Visit our website (www.MismatchedandThriving.com) and
print out "The Letter to My Chosen Mother." Write your
name on the letter. Read it out loud now, and then tuck it
into your Bible. Read it often, and allow the Lord to affirm
you, Mom.

Prayer

*O Lord Almighty God, Your ways are not our ways, yet You allow me to
see glimpses of You in my life and in the lives of my children. Your ways
are so much better than I could conceive. Thank You, Lord, for Your
relentless care, covering and pro-tection over my children.*

*Father, this is my humble prayer from the heart of a mother: Bring
my children into a rich and vibrant love relationship with You, and
Your Son, Jesus. Teach them to live empowered lives through the Holy
Spirit. Help me to be a living example to my kids, their father and the
world. Give me opportunities to share Your hope, to be merciful and
kind, to stand for Your truth.*

*Thank You for the gift of my children. Thank You that You love
them more than I do. Watch over them, speak wisdom into them,
protect and guide them all the days of their lives, and deliver them home
to heaven one day. And, Lord, it is my earnest desire that one day they
will be carriers of this faith legacy and bring the Good News to the next
generation. In the life-changing and redeeming name of Jesus, I ask all
these things. Amen.*

Respecting Dad

Not much is said in Scripture about the relationship of Eunice to her Greek husband. However, I would like to think that she loved him with the love of God. So, as we raise our children to know Christ, we can make every effort to fully love their father. As God's Word says, love covers a multitude of sins, and we can be assured that our love and prayers are far more powerful, persuasive and soothing than an unbelieving dad's convictions.

Trust God with your mismatched relationship and with your children. Mom, you do your part, and join God as He does His.

Conclusion

The End of a Story

Lynn

I ambled down the paper-goods aisle at the grocery store recently, just as I have hundreds of times before. It had been a nondescript, mundane day like so many others, until I reached up and pulled from a shelf a package of brown paper lunch bags. And it was in this precise moment, as I stared at the package of brown bags in my hand, that this innocuous day became quite profound.

Holding the bags, my mind raced. I had packed what seemed like a million lunches in brown paper bags over the years for both my kids. I'd been a mom with kids in the house for a very long time, but this package of bags changed everything. You see, this was the *last* package of bags I would ever buy to be filled with chips, apple slices and love. My daughter would graduate from high school before I could use up all these bags. Staring at the brown bags, a lump formed in my throat. I was oblivious to the rushing world of shoppers passing me by. Right there in the grocery store, I was overtaken by a feeling of melancholy. I gulped back tears and searched my purse for tissues. *Sniff . . . sniff.*

My long season of parenting was ending.

Finally, I gathered my feelings together, placed the package of bags in my cart and rolled on down the aisle. None of the other shoppers noticed my brimming tears. I whispered a quick prayer to my Abba Daddy and asked Him to watch over my babies.

That moment was the catalyst—silly brown paper bags—by which I started to ponder and to ask myself and God some of the scary questions I think we all contemplate as believing parents: Did I do it right? Did I do enough? Would growing up in a house in which her dad had never come to faith affect my daughter's faith in Jesus as an adult? Am I enough? Would my child go to heaven?

My friend, I wasn't a perfect parent. No one is! But I loved my children, I loved my husband, and I loved my Lord God and His Son, Jesus, and the Holy Spirit. And that was what I was supposed to do. Love will cover all those questions of doubt and guesses about whether or not I had been enough. The love of Christ fills in the empty spaces, and it's always enough.

Once we become a parent, we will always be a parent. As I type this closing, I await the birth of my first grandchild, a granddaughter, who will come any day now. My son and his wife are ecstatic. So am I. As parents, we never stop loving and praying for our family and for the next generation. Our legacy as mothers is priceless, and we will see the rewards of our love and faith in heaven as the generations arrive there, one by one, to say that their mother's faith was the most important part of their lives.

Finally, as we come to the end of this book, I want to share with you the ending to the story I began in chapter 2. If you remember, my daughter has been in the season of contemplating her choice for college in the fall. I had hoped I would be able to share her decision as we neared the end of this journey. I'm humbled to announce that my daughter made her choice to enroll this fall at BIOLA University—Bible Institute of Los Angeles—a Christian University.

Thank you for traveling this parenting journey with Dineen and me. I fall to my knees with overwhelming thanks and praise. I will forever tell everyone who will listen that God loves His children, that God is good and that our God is faithful.

As a precious mother, you are treasured, favored and esteemed in the eyes of God. Your high and noble calling will bring faith to the generations, and your life greatly honors the Lord Jesus Christ.

Thank you for spending time with Dineen and me. We love you. We really love you.

For the Lord is good. His unfailing love continues forever, and his faithfulness continues to each generation (Ps. 100:5, *NLT*).

Rebellion and the Prodigal Adult

Lynn

"Mom, I don't want to go."

I stood staring at my daughter's small face glaring back at me with pinched determination, her arms crossed in a defiant stance. In that moment I felt a panic creep up my neck, followed by a twinge of fear; but mostly a great disappointment overwhelmed me.

My daughter was entering into middle school, and for months I'd excitedly expected that she would join the middle-school youth group that met on Wednesday nights at church. My mention to her that youth group would be held that evening had brought about this unexpected reply.

I gathered myself.

Later that afternoon, after I'd had time to think, I talked with Caitie. I listened to her objections, which were valid. I insisted, however, that she give youth group a try. After all, she had yet to attend a meeting. I assured her that it would turn out to be fun. I asked her to commit to attending for the fall season, from the start of the school year through December, and if she still didn't want to attend at the end of the year, I would be completely fine with her decision to quit. She agreed.

December arrived. My daughter's report? "Mom, I'm done."

I honored my promise and released her from attending youth group. This scenario repeated itself with church camp, Sunday morning youth church and a number of other church youth events. Ugh! How I longed for her to be involved with other teenaged believers, but in our house, it just wasn't to be.

I will state here, however, that attending church on Sunday mornings was never negotiable.

But what do we do when our kids rebel against church, against our beliefs, and turn completely away from a life lived for Christ?

Regarding my daughter's choice to forgo youth group, I felt that she had made an earnest effort to participate. She invited her best friend to go with her, who attended most of the meetings that fall. However, when she shared with me her reasons for her decision, her explanations were reasonable and honest. I was compelled to trust her decision and to trust God that Sunday mornings would be sufficient for my daughter's spiritual training.

Parenting with love, grace and authority means walking a fine line. Balancing between our desires and our children's is at times a challenge, and it increases in difficulty as our kids become teens and young adults. For me, continuing to force my daughter to attend youth group would have birthed in her a resentment to all things of faith. I know my daughter well, and for most of her life she has been painfully shy. Her comfort in church on Sunday mornings exists because I'm by her side. Imposing my will on her to make her endure something that she disliked could have developed hatred in her, leaving a lifelong impact on her adult faith.

In the end, out of my love and respect for Caitie's well-thought-out decision, it was right for me to relent in order to preserve my daughter's relationship with Jesus.

However, what do you do when little Johnny isn't little anymore. Now he's 15 years old, 6 foot 2, 180 pounds and keenly aware that his father stays home every Sunday to pay homage to the NFL. One Sunday he casually says in reply to your question as to why he's not ready for church, "I'm staying home with Dad to watch football."

To complicate matters, Dad chimes in, "Let the kid stay home and watch the game."

I know women who have been stunned into blinding pain by this kind of exchange. But, my friends, I want to encourage you not to panic. God will not fail you, even if your kid decides to stay home every Sunday from that day forward. Nor will He fail you if your son or daughter purposely makes choices counter to God's will and in contrast to the truth of the Bible that are destructive, even evil, in nature.

I'm convinced that if we have prayed for our children and have lived out our vibrant faith in front of their eyes day in and day out, our example, our love and the love of Christ will resurface in them later in life.

I acknowledge there is real pain when a child chooses a rebellious and prodigal path. But our first step of action in learning to cope is to acknowledge our pain, disappointment and fear and then to immediately take these thoughts and emotions to God in prayer. Tell God that you are hurt, fearful and heartbroken. Lay your child at the foot of the throne every day in prayer.

Never stop praying for your children's return to the Father.

Dry Bones

I shared in my story at the beginning of this book that I was a good kid. But I later spent a string of years as a prodigal, far from the God I had been taught to know. So I can tell you that even good kids choose to turn away from their faith. But I'm convinced that my return to God was brought about for two reasons.

One, the Lord of the universe, His Son, Jesus, and the Holy Spirit relentlessly pursued me with a powerful, redemptive love.

Two, my mother prayed and never gave up hope. She was my soft landing spot, even when I had screwed up my life and the lives of others. She always listened to me. She loved me even when I refused to follow her gentle words of wisdom. She was always an example to me of living faith and joy. In the darkest points of my prodigal wanderings, my mother always, always loved me. She affirmed me in a way that bridged the gap between her pain and my arrogance.

I called my mother to ask her for the first time what she had prayed during the years of my Nebuchadnezzar insanity (see Dan. 4). Before she told me, she reminded me that she had tried to help me see that I would regret the decisions I was making. She also acknowledged that she had felt hopeless as I politely listened to her but ignored her advice.

Ouch!

However, she added that she had never felt as if God had abandoned me or that He had ignored her pleas on my behalf. Mom told me, "I prayed with fervor for your protection from evil people and from evil spirits. I begged God to help you make some intelligent decisions, and mostly I prayed, 'Lord, don't let go of her.'"

My friend, God will bring to bear His great power and love in the lives of those for whom we pray. He is a God of redemption—He wants to redeem our lost kids and also our unbelieving spouses. We are called to trust with unwavering faith that God will save our lost loved ones.

Believe God with such conviction that you become completely certain there is no other alternative except for God to fulfill His promises. Our God moves heaven and earth to meet expectations and prayers such as these. Then watch and wait for the miracles. God gives life to dry bones:

> "This is what the Sovereign LORD says: Come, O breath, from the four winds! Breathe into these dead bodies so they may live again."
>
> So I spoke the message as he commanded me, and breath came into their bodies. They all came to life and stood up on their feet—a great army.
>
> Then he said to me, "Son of man, these bones represent the people of Israel. They are saying, 'We have become old, dry bones—all hope is gone. Our nation is finished.' Therefore, prophesy to them and say, 'This is what the Sovereign LORD says: O my people, I will open your graves of exile and cause you to rise again. Then I will bring you back to the land of Israel. When this happens, O my people, you will know that I am the LORD. *I will put my Spirit in you, and you will live again and return home* to your own land. Then you will know

that I, the LORD, have spoken, and I have done what I said. Yes, the *Lord* has spoken!'" (Ezek. 37:9-14, *NLT*, emphasis added).

God's Intercessors

The Lord is not slow in keeping his promise, as some understand slowness. Instead he is patient with you, not wanting anyone to perish, but everyone to come to repentance.

2 PETER 3:9

It's difficult for me to imagine that God loves my children more than I do. I can only catch a glimpse of this understanding through the love relationship I have with God. I am a living example of the lengths our King Jesus will go to in order to redeem and to save one person from their self-destruction. God loves His people, and He will do whatever it takes to bring about our salvation. Jesus says in Luke 4,

> The Spirit of the Lord is on me, because he has anointed me to proclaim good news to the poor. He has sent me to proclaim freedom for the prisoners and recovery of sight for the blind, to set the oppressed free, to proclaim the year of the Lord's favor (vv. 18-19).

This is Jesus' mission and purpose, and it's ours as well. God partners with us, and especially with us moms, to release His power, love and intervention into the lives of those for whom we pray. We are to persevere in prayer, trusting that God is working all things out for our good, our children's good and His glory. We must pray with faith born of conviction that God's love and favor are upon our children. We must worship and praise God for the work He has done in our lives and in our children's lives. And finally, we must armor up, because we are at war. It's our words of intercession that can literally keep our children from the devil's grip.

I will tell you that our kids' freewill and their life choices will counter our prayers. However, over time God will reveal

Himself to our children over and again, offering them another chance at freedom.. One day He will break through.

I was delightfully surprised that on the very day that I was writing this about rebellious and prodigal children, I received an email from an old friend of mine whom I haven't heard from in a long, long time. She wrote,

> Last Sunday, the Lord gave me a front row seat as He brought His daughter, my eldest daughter, back home.
>
> As a mother of a prodigal, there is nothing in this life sweeter than to witness her rebirth. Her birth was wonderful—but the birthing of her new life was extraordinary.
>
> Perhaps you are the parent of a prodigal whom you have prayed for, and you feel there's not much hope . . . can I tell you something?
>
> Please keep praying.
>
> Your prodigal has a day . . . set and ordered by the Lord.
>
> If you think that it will happen in one particular way, please give up your idea to Him, and let Him do the orchestrating of the music of that life. He has written the most beautiful score to be heard—and only He knows when it will be played.
>
> My day came quite unexpectedly in some ways, but then totally expected in others. Take heart, parents. Keep praying. Your prodigal is still being watched by an Almighty eye. —Angie Knight

Mom, our message throughout this journey has been that we are to love the Lord our God with all our heart and with all our soul and with all our strength and with all our mind (see Luke 10:27). This kind of love relationship empowers us to live in the freedom of Christ. It will cause God's love to fill us up so completely that His love will overflow from us and splash onto our families and our lost loved ones. This kind of love transforms marriages, heals broken hearts, comforts and restores hurting children, and overcomes every single obstacle that the enemy sends our way.

Every word you whisper or even shout in prayer impacts the spiritual realm. Persevere in *faith*, never give up *hope*, and love with the *love* of Christ.

And now these three remain: faith, hope and love. But the greatest of these is love (1 Cor. 13:13).

Scripture Index: My Identity in Christ

Dineen

The Spirit of the Lord is on me, because he has anointed me to preach good news to the poor. He has sent me to proclaim freedom for the prisoners and recovery of sight for the blind, to release the oppressed, to proclaim the year of the Lord's favor.

LUKE 4:18-19

My friend, take your time and work through this list of Scripture verses that are not only for your children but for you as well. So many of us walk through life without fully understanding that we belong totally and completely to Jesus and that in Him we are new creations with completely new identities. Jesus doesn't make us clean up our act first either. In fact, He came specifically to set the prisoners and captives free, meeting people right where they are. That means you and me and everyone we love and meet.

You are:

- A citizen of heaven (Eph. 2:6; Phil. 3:20)
- A friend of God (John 15:14-15)
- A joint heir with Christ (Rom. 8:17, *NKJV*)
- A new creation (2 Cor. 5:17)
- A soldier (2 Tim. 2:3-4)
- Able to do all things through Christ (Phil. 4:13)

- Accepted (Rom. 15:7)
- Adequate (2 Cor. 3:5, *NASB*)
- Adopted as God's child (Eph. 1:5)
- An overcomer (1 John 5:4-5)
- Beautiful (Song of Songs 1:15)
- Beloved (Deut. 33:12)
- Bold and confident (Eph. 3:12, *NKJV*)
- Bought with a price and belonging to God (1 Cor. 6:20)
- Cherished (Ps. 83:3)
- Chosen (Col. 3:12)
- Christ's Bride (Rev. 21:9)
- Complete in Christ (Col. 2:10, *NASB*)
- Dead to sin and alive to God (Rom. 6:11)
- Delivered (2 Cor. 1:9-10)
- Encouraged (2 Thess. 2:16-17)
- Equipped (2 Tim. 3:17)
- Established, anointed and sealed by God (2 Cor. 1:21-22, *NASB*)
- Favored (Ps. 84:11)
- Given power, love and a sound mind (2 Tim. 1:7)
- God's child (John 1:12; Rom. 8:14-16)
- God's fellow worker (1 Cor. 3:9; 2 Cor. 6:1)
- God's holy people (Eph. 1:1)
- God's witness (Acts 1:8)
- God's workmanship (Eph. 2:10)
- Hidden with Christ in God (Col. 3:3)
- Holy (Heb. 10:10)
- Inscribed on the palm of God's hand (Isa. 49:16, *NKJV*)
- Justified (1 Cor. 6:11; Rom. 5:1)
- Known (Ps. 139:1)
- Made by God (Ps. 100:3)
- Made righteous (2 Cor. 5:21)
- Never forsaken (Heb. 13:5)
- One with God (John 17:23, *NKJV*)
- Perfect and complete (Jas. 1:2-4, *NKJV*)
- Prayed for (Rom. 8:27)
- Qualified to share Christ's inheritance (Col. 1:12)
- Redeemed (Gal. 3:13; Col. 1:14)

- Renewed (2 Cor. 4:16)
- Spiritually minded (Rom. 8:6)
- Sure that all things work together for good (Rom. 8:28)
- The light of the world (Matt. 5:14)
- The salt of the earth (Matt. 5:13)
- The temple of the Holy Spirit (1 Cor. 3:16; 6:19)
- Unable to be separated from God's love (Rom. 8:35-37)
- Under no condemnation (Rom. 8:1)
- United with the Lord and one spirit with Him (1 Cor. 6:17)
- Valued (Matt. 6:26)
- Victorious (1 Cor. 15:57)
- Washed, sanctified and justified (1 Cor. 6:11)

Prayers for Moms and Prayers for Our Kids

Prayers for You, Our Fellow Moms

God, equip this mother with the diligence to go to You on behalf of her children. When she is in doubt of the power she possesses, remind her that You have entrusted her with these precious ones and that she herself brings holiness to her home and to her children. God, remind her of the battle that wages for her children. Help her to remember that all You ask of her is that she be faithful and diligent to "train up a child in the way he should go" (Prov. 22:6). Release her from any fear of her children's choices as adults. Let her not fear what the future may hold but let her hang on to the fact that she has the ability to make an impact on her kids through her example and through her precious prayers as a mother. Give this mom a verse to remind her of what You have called her to do.

When she doubts her role, flood her with reminders through Scripture, friends and encouragement to fight the good fight! Remind her that she is a seed planter and that the godly people You bring into her children's lives are the ones who will water, and that You will grow them into what You have called them to be.

—SHELLY WEAVER

My Abba Father, I pray with an overflowing and earnest heart for every mother who loves You and who loves her children that she will find encouragement in Your presence. Lord, fill her up with energy on her difficult days. Reveal to her the great value of her efforts regularly so that she will maintain her focus and will continue the mission You have decreed for her. Speak gentle words of love to her when she is scared, worried, tired or hormonal. Lord, surround her with Your people to speak wisdom, laughter and hope into her as a mother.

Father, from this day forward let this beautiful and precious mother never forget that her high and holy calling surpasses all others in her life, and remind her that she will have a lasting impact on the world through her offspring for generations to come.

Protect her from the lies of the enemy. Bless her with provision, abundance and delight. Let her see the love notes that You send to her every day. Fill her life with adventure, laughter, promise, skills, unending energy and a will to serve You and her family with the love of Christ. Show her how very proud of her You are, and let her walk fully in her God-given identity as a child of the Most High God.

—LYNN DONOVAN

Prayers for Our Children

Lord, I pray that You would handpick every one of my children's friends, that each one would be loyal and honest and would walk with integrity so as to be a good influence on my kids. I pray that my children will be a good influence on their friends as well—the presence and aroma of Christ. If any friend in my children's lives is a negative or evil influence, please change this person's heart or take this person out of my kids' lives. Lord, help my children to treat their friends with kindness, respect and consideration. Help them to walk with integrity of heart, as David did.

—DINEEN MILLER

This is what I pray on the nights when I put my young boys to bed:

Dear Lord, thank You for _____, _____ and _____.
Thank You for Your love for them and Your special plan for

each of their lives. Please bless them and keep them, and lead them all their days. May they always know Your great love for them.

The last line I find especially important. That is the one thing everything hinges on, because it is when we lose sight of how much God loves us that we tend to fall away from Him. But even when life's not fun, if we can still feel His love, it makes all the difference.

—GILLIAN RUSSELL MEISNER

I like to pray Ephesians 1:16-20:

I thank God for you. I pray for you, _____ , constantly, asking God, the glorious Father of our Lord Jesus Christ, to give you, _____ , spiritual wisdom and insight so that you, _____ , might grow in your knowledge of God. I pray that your heart will be flooded with light so that you, _____ , can understand the confident hope God has given to those He has called—His holy people, who are His rich and glorious inheritance. I also pray that you, _____ , will understand the incredible greatness of God's power for us who believe in Him. This is the same mighty power that raised Christ from the dead and seated Him in the place of honor at God's right hand in the heavenly realms.

—DEBRA ALLEY

Father God, may my children fall in love with You.

—MARTHA BUSH

Dear Lord, I pray that You would keep a constant hedge of protection around these children and that You would keep the evil one far from them. Lord, I also pray that You would give me a vision for my children's future so I can cooperate with You in the plans You have for them. In Jesus' name. Amen.

—TAMARA HAJCAK

Dear Lord, heavenly Father, thank You for these children whom You have entrusted to me. Help my children to rely on You at all times; help them to be saved. May they put You first in their lives. Whatever Your will is for their lives is what we want. Help us all to love each other and to embrace Your will for our lives. Help us to appreciate each gift You have given us in our personalities and in our lives. In Jesus' name. Amen.

—ANDREA LUDWIG

Lord, prepare my child's future spouse, and build a firm and unshakable foundation of faith in this person who will marry my child. I ask for this same preparation for my child so that, as You have designed for marriage, the two of them will become one, will walk together in strong faith and, by serving each other and others, will bring You glory, Father. Keep them both pure until the day of marriage. Until they meet, guard their hearts and remove any romantic entanglement from their lives that is counter to Your plan of what's best for them. Help them both to be patient and to trust You to bring them together according to Your perfect timing.

—DINEEN MILLER

Lord, please fill my daughter to overflowing with Your Holy Spirit. From her young age may she be used for Your kingdom's purposes; may she learn to pray to You and to see and know Your answers to her prayer; may she learn to hear and know Your voice. Keep her safe. Give her wisdom in school and in her studies, and please prepare a godly husband for her in the future so that she will not have to walk the path that I have walked. In Jesus' name. Amen.

—OLGA G.

Father, guide my children to always love unconditionally, even when they mess up or experiment—because all kids do. Amen.

When your children disappoint you, ask God for guidance, and ask Him to restore your unconditional love toward them.

—GAIL McKINNEY

Father, please give me the strength not to get in Your way in my children's lives so that they become all that You have planned for them. Help me to share Your love, Your mercy and Your grace with them and to point them toward You when they are wandering away, confused or scared. Help me to love my kids when they are not very loveable, to see what You see, to say what You'd say. Help me to know that it's not all about what I want them to become but what You desire for them, so that they will bring glory to You and will be Your hands and feet in this broken world.

—Jen Babcock

Thank You, Lord Jesus, that You daily walk with my children, that You daily plan for my children's futures and that You have designed my children uniquely for their generation to be Your light in this world. Release Your full potential in them, and show them daily how to walk in it, Holy Spirit. In Your name, Jesus, I pray this for each of my children. Amen.

—Dineen Miller

Abba Father, I'm placing my children in the palm of Your hand this very hour. I ask You to anoint my children with a fire so that they will live a fulfilling life in Your presence. Place in these children a hunger for more of You and for Your purposes for their lives. Reveal in tender love the true character traits You instilled into my children. Empower my children to step into their destinies with the courage of Joshua and Caleb. Create opportunities daily for them to witness Your love in action, Your grace in great measure and Your forgiveness that brings freedom. Then place these qualities into their hearts, and let them live there forever.

Walk with my children today, revealing to them Your power and purpose. Let my children live in the freedom of their true identity in Christ, and encourage them to step into the authority and privilege of royalty. Perfect their destinies.

Bring them joy in everyday living, peace to share with the world, love that overcomes all evil and a light that changes the atmospheres in which they walk. Shine in them so brightly that thousands are brought home to You. Lord, may my children become all that You desire and may they bring great honor, glory and power to Your name. I ask in the name of King Jesus. Amen.

—Lynn Donovan

Scripture Prayers We Can Pray for Our Children

Psalm 4:3 (*NKJV*): "But know that the Lord has set apart for Himself him who is godly."

My child has been set apart to serve You, Lord. Help me as a mother to see my child as holy and destined for great things in Your kingdom. Help me to gently guide my child in Your ways.

John 1:12: "Yet to all who did receive him, to those who believed in his name, he gave the right to become children of God."

Lord, my child is Your child. Please reveal Yourself to my child in ways that he or she will receive salvation and will thrive in this life.

Ephesians 4:32: "Be kind and compassionate to one another, forgiving each other, just as in Christ God forgave you."

Lord, help me to model kindness and compassion and to instill these qualities into my child. I ask that these qualities will guide my child in all his or her relationships.

Jeremiah 15:16 (*NLT*): "When I discovered your words, I devoured them. They are my joy and my heart's delight, for I bear your name, O Lord God of Heaven's Armies."

Place in my children a hunger for Your holy Word, and may the Scriptures be the wisdom and truth that lead them all their lives.

Proverbs 13:20: "Walk with the wise and become wise."

Lord Almighty, let my children choose their friends wisely. Keep them from the influence of people who appear to offer friendship but who will lead them away from You. Lord, surround my children with friendships that are honorable, sincere, kind and fruitful. Let a genuine love and commitment rise out of these friendships that are centered in You. This is my plea from a mother's heart.

Ephesians 6:10: "Finally, be strong in the Lord and in his mighty power."

Almighty Father, surround my children with Your protection. Help me to teach them to place their armor on as they walk into the world. Make them strong in the Lord, and may they live in the authority and power You intend them to. When they battle evil, go before them and lead them to victory and peace.

Luke 2:52: "And Jesus grew in wisdom and stature, and in favor with God and man."

Abba Daddy, I humbly ask that my children grow up learning the value of wisdom. Bless them with Your wisdom. Grant them the discernment and wisdom that the world doesn't understand. Let my children see circumstances and opportunities through the lens of the Bible. And because You have graced my children with great wisdom, let them humbly grow in great favor with man and even more so in Your great favor.

Psalm 37:4: "Take delight in the LORD and he will give you the desires of your heart."

Great King, this verse is the desire of my mother's heart. May my children take such great delight in You that they find their way through this life with joy, experience Your lavish love daily and receive riches unending. May they delight in You, and as they do, I pray that You will bless them with every desire of their heart.

Bringing Faith Home: Family-Faith Traditions and Projects

Charities
(Dineen)

Almost every Christmas, my youngest daughter, Leslie, and I find special goodies with which to fill a shoebox-sized container for Operation Christmas Child. We also support two World Vision children year-round, one of whom my daughter picked and contributed part of her allowance to. Doing these kinds of things can be a great way to help our children develop a sense of connection and a heart for others in need. Have your kids join you in selecting a child to support. Our special kids share the same birthday month as my girls. Getting the reports from these children and seeing them thrive has been profoundly rewarding for us.

Heart Attack
(Lynn)

One year for Valentine's Day I cut out pink-, purple-, white- and rose-colored hearts from construction paper—about 20 of them. The hearts were about three inches across. With a Sharpie I wrote down on each heart one of the qualities or characteristics that I love about my daughter. I wrote, "You are beautiful," "You love Jesus," "You are a good friend," "You are a great student," "You love animals," "You are smart," "You are funny," etc. After my daughter went to bed, I taped the hearts to her door. When she woke in the morning, she received a heart attack that filled her heart with love. I also did this for my spouse. The hearts hung on my daughter's and my husband's doors for more than a year.

Resurrection Eggs
(Lynn)

I shared the story in chapter 3 about how every Easter we pull out the carton of Family Life's Resurrection Eggs and reenact the story of the Passion Week through the contents of the egg. A family favorite.

Chocolate Crosses
(Dineen)

As a kid, I loved getting an Easter basket full of goodies each year. I wanted to carry on this family tradition with my kids, but I wanted to make it about Jesus too. I don't know which candy company started making chocolate crosses, but I'm so glad they did. Every year my girls received a small chocolate bunny *and* a chocolate cross. Most drugstores carry them, but shop early, because they seem to go fast. Gee, imagine that.

Tablecloth of Thanks
(Lynn)

When my daughter was young, I threw a pristine, white tablecloth across our dining room table the first week in November. I gave my daughter a color-fast pen and said, "Write your thanks right on this tablecloth." At first, of course, she thought I was nuts, but she picked up the pen and scribbled out something completely cute for a little girl. I then told her to sign her name and to write the year, 2006. Every year since then we have placed this tablecloth in the dining room, and each family member writes what he or she is thankful for that year. Guests have shared their blessings in this way, and even one of our dogs added his thanks! I don't know how he grew fingers, but he wrote that he was thankful for dog bones. *grin.*

This tablecloth has become our favorite holiday tradition in our home. It is a powerful witness to my husband, and it shouts of God's love and favor for the rich blessings He pours out upon our home.

Thankful Jar
(Liz, a Reader)

I have a "thankful jar" that sits on the living-room table year round. All year my family members add notes to the jar on which are written things that we are thankful for. On Thanksgiving we pull out the pieces of paper and read them. A few weeks after the holiday, I paste all the notes into an annual "thankful journal" so that I will be able to keep the kids' thoughts, thanks and handwriting forever.

Christmas Quilt Calendar
(Dineen)

I remember as a child counting the days down to Christmas with Hershey Chocolate Kisses. My mother would purchase a calendar that had a kiss attached to each day leading up to the twenty-fifth, much like the chocolate advent calendars we see each year.

This became my inspiration one year to create a calendar for my girls. I did a lot of quilting at the time, and I found a great tree pattern. I used it to create the calendar and then made a pocketed border on three sides of the tree. On each pocket I painted the day of the month, except for the pocket for the thirteenth (Leslie's birthday), the twentieth (Rachel's birthday) and the twenty-fifth (Jesus' birthday). On each of those I painted the birthday person's name. Then in each pocket I put a miniature ornament for the girls to hang on a tree in the center of the calendar (they hung the ornaments on tiny bells that I had sewn into the fabric) and a wrapped chocolate treat.

To this day my girls love this calendar, and even as adults they insist that I hang it up and load the pockets with ornaments and chocolates. The ornaments have been changed periodically through the years, but the tiny baby Jesus in His manger remains the pinnacle of the calendar and sits atop the tree.

Kids love things like this, and with these kinds of traditions comes the chance to remind them all December long of the true meaning of Christmas.

Advent Wreath
(Dineen)

Another family tradition that we love in our home during the holiday season is an Advent wreath. If you do an Internet search on this, you will discover various adaptations and ideas for this project. I fell in love with this tradition while at our church in Zürich, and I kept it simple for my family at home. Just a green wreath (fake or real) with four purple or burgundy candles around the outside to count down each of the four Sundays in Advent (in December) and a white center candle for the Christ child to be lit on Christmas day. Each year the hunt for this special center candle became part of our tradition as we looked for a candle worthy of the baby Jesus, our Savior. We would even pray for God to lead us to one decorated with sparkles and glitter in honor of Jesus. Each Sunday as we lit a candle, we talked about a specific Scripture that had to do with hope, joy, peace or love, always ending our talk on the final Sunday with the theme of love.

The Jesus Box
(Dineen)

Find a special box, or decorate one with your kids. As Christmas approaches, ask your children to think about what gift they would like to give Jesus (as a birthday present). This is a conceptual gift, of course, so give your children some ideas to get them started. Suggest things such as making a commitment to read one Bible verse every day, to not talk back to mom, or to make a new kid at school feel welcome. Have your kids write down their special gift idea and put it in the box, and then place the box under the tree on Christmas Day. Each year, before you place your new "gifts" in the box, let your kids read what they wrote the year before. It's a great way to talk to them about spiritual growth and about the importance of keeping our commitments to God.

The Jesus Cake/Happy Birthday Jesus Party
(Dineen)

I first heard of this when I was living in Memphis, Tennessee, and I was delighted to see it in Europe as well. Again, search online for "Jesus birthday cake." You'll find ideas for throwing a complete birthday party. But the cake is my favorite part of this idea, because each layer is colored to represent some aspect of Jesus, and the icing and decorations incorporate the reason for His birth and His death as well. Throw a party with your children for baby Jesus, and have fun!

Nativity Scenes
(Dineen)

This may be a tradition you already hold dear. My girls loved setting up the Nativity scene each year. During our first Christmas in Europe, I noticed that a friend's Nativity scene was missing the baby Jesus. I asked her what had happened to Him. She explained that it was a tradition for them to hide the baby Jesus and that the children had to find Him on Christmas morning and return Him to the manger. How symbolic of finding our salvation in Jesus!

Leader's Guide
Small Group Study

Lynn and Dineen

*The greatest among you will be your servant. For those
who exalt themselves will be humbled, and those
who humble themselves will be exalted.*

MATTHEW 23:11-12

Leading a small group is one of the most rewarding investments
you will make in the kingdom of God. Thank you for giving
your time, love and prayers to help others discover hope for
their children. Dineen and I have prayed for you, asking the
Lord to bless you as you facilitate this study.

Helpful Hints as You Begin

- Love on the ladies who are in your group. Make them
  feel welcomed and comfortable.
- Listen more and talk less. Keep confidences. Encourage
  the women to share, and assure them that your study
  is a safe place in which they are free to be authentic.
- Encourage uplifting talk of husbands and dads, and
  let the women know that your group is not a place for
  husband or father bashing.
- Encourage each member of your group to speak.
  Although some individuals share more easily than

others, these ladies sometimes dominate conversations. Steer the conversation to allow everyone a chance to contribute to it. Thank those who share frequently, then ask someone who is quiet to share her thoughts.

- Always use the Bible as the basis for truth in your group. Encourage women to search out and to provide Scriptures to support their opinions.
- Use discernment, share your heart with authenticity and allow yourself to be vulnerable without making the group uncomfortable.
- Be sensitive to your members' time. Begin the study on time, and end on time.
- Invite the Holy Spirit into your group, and expect the love of Christ to transform lives.
- If at any time you feel that any member of your group or her children may be exposed to abuse or addiction, encourage her to seek professional Christian counseling. Seek wise counsel from your church pastor as well.
- Visit www.MismatchedandThriving.com for free handouts and study support materials that can be used at any time in your group study.

Sessions

This is an 11-week study. It includes one introduction session, followed by a review of each of the 10 chapters of *Not Alone*. During the week leading up to your first meeting, cover your study and the women who will be attending it with prayers of protection, and ask the Lord for a fresh anointing of the Holy Spirit. Also, telephone each participant, introduce yourself as the group leader and remind the ladies of the meeting date and time and other pertinent details. Let them know that you are praying for them. Share your excitement over what God has prepared for your group.

As the group leader, greet the women as they arrive each week. Begin the meetings on time, and remind the women to silence their cellular phones. After your first introductory meeting, the basis for your meetings each week will be the "Discovery" sections at the end of each chapter in this book. As your group discusses the discovery questions, allow for differences of opinion in your discussions, always pointing to Scripture as the final truth. Remember to have a box of tissue close by.

Any study that deals with personal issues such as marriage and parenting will require discernment and sensitivity on the part of the leader. Be aware that some women in your group will struggle with the concept (or label) of being mismatched. You can also expect to have women join your group who, although their husbands are professed believers, may be uncertain of their spouses' faith condition. And welcome with open arms women who are divorced and single mothers. Make each one welcome regardless of her spouse's faith. Your group was hand selected by God, and you can expect Him to change lives.

Thank you for giving of yourself to others for the glory of God.

"His master replied, 'Well done, good and faithful servant!'" (Matt. 25:23).

Introduction: Your First Meeting

- Consider having beverages available, as well as nametags. Also have copies of the Member Class Form (at the end of this book) prepared to hand out.
- Welcome the women, and get to know them as they arrive.
- Begin the meeting with prayer.
- Introduce yourself, and introduce your family by sharing a photo of them. Share some information about each of your children, such as his or her name, age and basic interests, and share a fun or funny story about a parenting moment from your life. Provide the group with your name and phone number.
- Break the ice with something fun and easy. For example, play "In the Bag": Fill a purse with a variety of items, such as keys, nail polish, dental floss, a small Bible, a cross, a pacifier, a pack of tissues, a candy bar, a

cell phone, crayons, etc. Be creative. Give each woman the opportunity to place her hand in the purse for 15 seconds and, when the time is up, to write down as many items as she can remember feeling. The woman who remembers the most items wins a prize.

- Ask each attendee to share about her children's ages, genders, names, etc. Ask them to bring a photo of their children to next week's study if they don't have photos with them in their handbag.
- Review the schedule of your study—times, dates and other information, such as a snack schedule if applicable.
- Review the study format. As the group leader, we suggest that you highlight key concepts from the chapter and discuss these. Then review the study questions with the group. Conclude with prayer. Ask the women for prayer requests. One way to do this would be to pass out 3x5 cards and have each woman write out her requests, then pass her card to the neighbor on her right so that the person can pray over her requests for the week.
- Remind your group why they are there: to study the Bible, to grow in their relationship with Christ, to build relationships with each other, to share and grow in a safe community in which they can encourage one another as mothers and, ultimately, to instill faith in Christ in their children.
- Make a copy of the Small Group Agreement (at the end of this book), and review it with the women.
- Have the ladies complete the Member Class Form and then turn it into the leader.
- Pass out the books, and assign the first chapter reading and questions that follow.
- Time permitting, ask the participants about their hopes and expectations regarding this study.
- Pray and then close the meeting.

Chapter 1: Extraordinary Kids

Be intentional about welcoming each woman as she comes in, and give hugs and smiles as needed. Sometimes newcomers can associate an overlooked greeting as a rejection or as a sign that they don't fit in.

Begin your session with prayer, inviting the Holy Spirit into your study group. Take a moment to share any family photos the women brought with them this week. Encourage the women to become familiar with each other's children and to pray for one another's families.

In this session you may want to offer an overview of the study's content. Review the discovery at the end of chapter 1, and encourage your participants, if they are comfortable, to share their answers. Consider sharing from your own experience to help create an atmosphere of camaraderie and trust within the group.

As this is the first session, be patient with the silences and sensitive to the fact that in this first week we tackle a very personal question, "Am I enough?" Encourage the women to share. Guide the conversation to uncover fears and anxieties, and instill truth in the ladies from God's Word.

Assign reading and questions for next week, and close with prayer.

Chapter 2: Heaven's Kids

Welcome returning members and any new members to your group. Begin your session with prayer. Ask the ladies to share their thoughts on the content and general theme of chapter 2. Explore together the truth that a mother's faith is the foundation of faith in her children. Discuss this concept.

Review the chapter's discovery questions, and look up 1 Corinthians 7:12-14 together. Discuss the concept of sanctification and how it can be applied in each of your homes. Encourage discussion as you move through the questions. If time permits, look up Proverbs 22:6 and discuss it. Share a prodigal story from your own life or have someone from the group share one to encourage the others.

Assign reading and questions for next week, and close with prayer.

Chapter 3: Equipped Kids

Begin your session with prayer. Ask the members of your group to share any changes and/or answers to their prayers, and ask them to share how praying for their children by name has changed their prayers.

Review the discovery questions for chapter 3. Focus on discussions about stepping into the role of spiritual leader in your home and how you can balance that with respecting your husband as leader in other areas of your life.

Share some teachable moments that you have experienced with your kids, and encourage the women to share their ideas for teachable moments with each other. Have someone write down some of these ideas and bring a handout with the ideas printed on it to next week's class.

This week, assign the women to pray that they will catch teachable moments with their kids, and challenge them to create at least one fun and spontaneous adventure with their children that will surprise and delight the kids.

Assign reading (include Appendix 1, "Rebellion and the Prodigal Adult") as well as questions for next week, and close with prayer.

Chapter 4: Churched Kids

Begin your session with prayer. Ask the women how they were intentional about creating teachable moments in their home this past week. Ask them to share their spontaneous adventure(s).

In this session ask the members to share some of their "getting to church" debacles and triumphs. Look up Hebrews 10:24-25, and discuss the passage. What are the biblical benefits of assembly with other believers?

Review the chapter 4 discovery questions. Approach the first question with sensitivity, as women who are doing this study with other members of their church may not want to talk openly about the church. Encourage women to seek God's wisdom and discernment regarding this question. Ask the group members to share their thoughts on how they can embrace the design of their mismatched family units at church. Help them to find freedom from preconceived expectations of a family unit at church.

Share within the group ideas to help children engage in church groups and events. Allow time as well for discussion of Appendix 1, "Rebellion and the Prodigal Adult." There may be mothers whose children are walking through a season of rebellion who will need encouragement in this season of life.

Assign reading and questions for next week, and close with prayer.

Chapter 5: Peaceful Kids

Begin your session with prayer. Be aware that opinions may differ greatly in this chapter about how many activities our children should be involved in and about which things we should say no to. As you review the discovery questions for chapter 5, encourage the women to share thoughts and re-sources regarding these issues.

Explore the concept of comparing what is good to what is God's best. Encourage your group to share ideas of how they are teaching and helping their children to make good choices at home, at school and when they're out with friends.

Look up Ephesians 4:14, and talk about what it means to speak the truth in love. Introduce TCWT—*truth, conviction, words* and *timing*—a method for approaching a loved one regarding an issue that needs to be discussed.

This process begins with praying for God to show you the *truth* of the situation. What is really going on? What is your responsibility and motivation in initiating this discussion? Then pray for *conviction* of heart for yourself and for the other person involved. Next pray for the *words* to speak to your loved one; and finally, pray for *timing* so that God will prepare your heart to speak in love and will prepare your loved one's heart to hear your words in truth and love.

Assign reading and questions for next week, and close with prayer.

Chapter 6: Generous Kids

Begin your session with prayer. Spend some time talking about the challenges of loving others, and encourage the group to believe that when we pray and ask God to love others through us, He will change our hearts. Review the discovery questions for chapter 6. Encourage stories of generosity, and as you hear them, give God the glory!

Look up 1 Thessalonians 5:23-24 and Hebrews 10:23. Ask the group how they see God's faithfulness working in their lives and in the lives of their children.

Consider a project that your group could undertake to help someone in the church or community or to help a cause. Be sensitive to time constraints, and try to pick options that will involve the women's children.

Assign reading and questions for next week, and close with prayer.

Chapter 7: Authentic Kids

Begin your session with prayer. Talk for a while about who we are in Christ, and ask the members to share at what level they feel they are walking in their identity in Christ: somewhat, getting there or embracing the full truth of who we are in Him. Discuss the chapter 7 discovery questions.

Look up 1 Corinthians 12:1-11 and Romans 12:6-8. If you feel your group is open to discussing spiritual gifts, ask them if they identify with any of the gifts mentioned. Also ask if they see some of these gifts in their children. Encourage the women who are unclear about this topic to pray for guidance and wisdom in this area, and even challenge them to ask God to release these gifts in their lives and in the lives of their children.

Encourage the group to share any stories of provision in which something came to them clearly at the hand of God.

Assign reading and questions for next week, and close with a prayer that Jesus will begin establishing the truths of who we are in Him in the heart of each woman there.

Prior to adjournment, plan for next week's lesson, which includes a Mexican food potluck (see chapter 8 lesson below).

Chapter 8: Triumphant Kids

Begin your session with prayer. Ask your members about their week.

In this session set the stage with a potluck of Mexican food, if it's appropriate for your study time and place. Enjoy tacos, and review the discovery questions for chapter 8 together. Share ideas on how to make your house "the home with the open door."

Assign reading and questions for next week, and close with prayer.

Chapter 9: Challenging Kids

Begin your session with prayer. Ask your members how they did with this week's chapter, which covers some tough areas. Try to stay very sensitive to the leading of the Holy Spirit, because this may be a time for some women in your group to open up about struggles they are having but haven't felt they could share openly in other venues. Have tissues and hugs ready!

Ask the group what they thought of Kendra's story. Review the discovery questions for chapter 9. Compile a list of ideas that the woman come up with from question number four, and make a handout to give to your group members the following week. These ideas may even spur more.

Encourage the women also to have a prayer partner or a mentor whom they can talk to and pray with as they walk through any trial or challenge they are facing with their child. If you as the leader know of women in your church who can step into this role, prayerfully consider how to help the ladies in your group make connections with these women.

Assign reading and questions for next week, and close with a prayer that God's strength will carry each woman through whatever challenges she is facing.

Chapter 10: Legacy Kids

Begin your session with prayer. Ask your members about their week. Discuss the chapter 10 discovery questions, and have someone in the group read aloud "The Letter to My Chosen Mother." Again, have tissues ready! *smile.*

In this session ask the members how their parenting perspectives have changed over the course of the study. Discuss the highlights that mothers have gained from this study. Ask the ladies to share the areas that they will continue to focus on in the weeks ahead.

Wrap up your study, and encourage each woman to simply grow in her love for Jesus and to allow that love to overflow to her children, to her husband and to a world in desperate need of a Savior. Close with prayer.

Member Class Form[*]

Name: _____

Address: _____

Phone: _____

E-mail: _____

Spouse's Name: _____

Children's names and ages: _____

What are you hoping to learn from this study?

_____

_____

_____

What is your greatest spiritual, physical or emotional challenge at this time?

_____

_____

_____

How can your group leader pray for you throughout this study?

_____

_____

_____

Questions you may have:

_____

_____

_____

* This form is supremely confidential. Your group leader will refer to it when she covers you and your family with prayer.

Small Group Agreement

I agree to . . .

Grow spiritually as an individual and as a group; to build a strong marriage through the application of biblical truth.

Give priority to the group meeting, arriving on time with reading and study questions complete.

Pray regularly for group members

Pray daily for my husband.

Be a safe place where women are free to be authentic and develop trust and godly relationships.

Keep confidences. What is said in the group stays in the group.

Be patient with others, offer love and stay clear of judgments.

Invite other women to join the group who would benefit from the study and prayer.

Laugh, love, cry and expect Jesus to show up.

Signed: _____

Date: _____

Lynn@mismatchedandthriving.com

Dineen@mismatchedandthriving.com

Our consuming desire is that every woman would walk in the freedom, authority and power of her inheritance in Jesus Christ. As women, when we walk in this truth, our lives are ignited by Holy Spirit fire, and we bring a legacy of faith for the generations to come. From our hearts to yours, our passion is to share these truths with women in a variety of settings such as conferences, retreats and small group events.

"Love...transparency...open eyes and more God and His Spirit than you could imagine or dream of! That is the package God sent with Lynn and Dineen to Rancho Community Church! My dream for our body of women was to experience God "out of the box." And we did through His divine anointing on them to be transparent and real. Lynn and Dineen are real women like you and me...but with bigger-than-this-life faith! They led us on a journey to dig out the junk God never intended for us to hold on to. As this played out, hands began to join, tears began to fall, and bondage was broken, leaving open spaces in our spirits for God to fill that day and beyond! God used these amazing ladies to begin a revival in our valley."

— Jodie Taylor, women's ministry organizer
Rancho Community Church - Temecula, California

"Lynn and Dineen are two extraordinary women of God. Our event was blessed with the Spirit of the Lord and with the joy and love these two women bring as they touch lives for God. Their vulnerability and love for women are tangible and life giving in the kingdom of God. And to see God speak into each and every woman's life who attended was a sweet surprise. Not only those who were fortunate enough to attend were blessed but also those women who read their books and blog.

I encourage women to not only read Lynn and Dineen's books but also to gather women around them into small groups to study God's word and the keys points of these books. Every marriage will be blessed."

— Mary Doering, pastor's wife
and women's ministry leader
Christ the King Community Church - Kingwood, Texas

"I confess the longevity of being in a 38 year old unequally yoked marriage is sometimes a discouragement to me, but getting back into God's presence, which was so real at this retreat, helped me to get my head on straight again. I can best describe what I encountered as a renewed JOY."

— Martha Bush, conference attendee
Orange, Texas

Mismatched & Thriving *Ministries*

Living with Purpose . . . Through Kingdom Power . . . and Transforming Faith

For more information on how to plan an event with Lynn and Dineen,
visit MismatchedandThriving.com